Air Fryer Cookbook

Affordable and Delicious Recipes for Everyone

Mark Smith

Table of Contents

Introduction 1

What Is an Air Fryer? 4
    Benefits of the Air fryer 4
    5 Tips for the Air fryer 5
    How to Clean the Air Fryer 5

Breakfast Recipes 7
    Hard Boiled Eggs with Spinach and Tomatoes 8
    Lemon Strawberry Corn Muffins 10
    Delicious Air Fryer Pancake with Raspberry Topping 12
    Breakfast Soufflé 13
    French toast 15
    Air Fryer Banana Bread 16
    Mushroom Omelet in Air Fryer 18
    Toad-In-The-Hole 19
    Breakfast Frittata 20
    Breakfast Tortilla Wraps 21

Quick Easy Recipes 22
    Bacon-Wrapped Potato Tots 23
    Mozzarella Sticks 24
    Garlic Coated Potato Wedges In Air Fryer 26
    Garlic Knots 28
    Spinach and Cheese Muffins 30
    Artichokes with Honey Dijon 31
    Simple Jicama Chip 33
    Stuffed Jalapeno Peppers 34
    Crispy Chicken Fingers with Ranch Dressing 35

Quick Pita Pizza 36

Chicken Recipes 37
Glazed Chicken Breast   with Basil Corn Salad 38
BBQ Chicken With Baked Potatoes 42
Pistachio Crusted Chicken 43
Cosmic Wings 44
BBQ Chicken Breasts With Coleslaw 47
Chicken Tomatina With Rice 48
Roasted Cinnamon Apple With The Chicken 50
Crispy Fillets With Sriracha Honey Sauce 51

Turkey Recipes 53
Turkey Croquettes 54
Turkey Sandwich Melt 56
Air Fryer Turkey Breast 58
Air Fryer Garlic Herb Turkey Breast 59
Juicy Air Fryer Turkey 60

Beef Recipe 61
Beef Tenderloin 62
Pear Bake Tri-Tip Steaks 64
Beef Milanese with Stuffed Mushrooms 66
Juicy Vegetables And Sirloin Steak With Sour Cream 68
Beef Stuffed Bell Peppers 69
Sticky Sweet Beef Ribs with Baked Potatoes 70
Air Fryer Rib Eye 72
Maple Glazed Rib Eye Steak 73
Chipotle New York Steak 74
Marinated Beef Roast 75

Lamb Recipes 77
Herbed and Garlic Lamb Rack 78
Raspberry Chipotle Lamb Chop 79
Mustard Lamb Chops With Chimichurri Sauce 81
Bourbon Lamb Chops With Baked Potatoes 83
Sticky Sweet Lamb Ribs 85

Fish Recipes 86
Steamed Salmon With Lemon And Herbs 87
Halibut with Vegetables 89
Pecan Sauce with Salmon 91
Mahi Fillets With Mango Salsa 93
Crispy Fish Fillets 95
Fish with Spicy Herb Vinaigrette 96
Cajun Salmon 98
Sweet Glazed Salmon 99
Sundried Tomato with Salmon 100
Salmon with Green Pesto Sauce 101

Shrimp Recipes 102
Bacon-Wrapped Buffalo Shrimp 103
Lemon Pepper Shrimp with Butter Sauce 104
Easy Popcorn Shrimp 106
Shrimp, Mushroom, and Broccoli 107
Simple Shrimp 108

Pizza Recipes 109
Crab Pizza 110
Chicken Pizza 112
Cheese and Broccoli Pizza 114
Eggplant Pizza 116

    All Cheese Pizza 117

Snacks And Bread 118
    Air Fried Tofu 119
    Potato Wedges 120
    Onion Rings 121
    Air-Fried Apple Chips 122
    Kale Chips 123

Vegetable Recipes 124
    Purple Medley 125
    Simple Jicama Chip 126
    Easy Ratatouille 127
    Air Fryer Vegetable Nuggets 128
    Tortillas Wraps 129
    Garlic Parmesan Asparagus 131
    Sesame and Balsamic Vinegar Green Beans 132
    Crispy Avocado Fries With Chipotle Kale Dip 133
    Spicy Herbed Zucchini Chips 135
    Coated Carrots Fries 136

Desserts 137
    Air Fryer S'Mores Dip 138
    Air Fryer Semolina Pudding 139
    Strawberry Cobbler in the Air Fryer 140
    Easy Chocolate Cake 141
    Chocolate Orange Cupcakes Recipe 143
    Air Fryer Strawberry & Cream Mug Cake 145
    Fruit Pudding 146
    Lemon Biscuits 147
    Walnut Chocolate Cookies 148

Chocolate Chip Cookie 149

NOTES **150**

Conclusion **151**

Introduction

This cookbook is about making some astonishingly easy air fryer recipes that are delicious and prepared with less effort. An air fryer is undoubtedly a magical appliance that works with a click of a button. An air fryer is a hot trending appliance that is also an efficient and energy-saving appliance.

Suppose you have a busy lifestyle that makes it hard to prepare a meal. Or you love cooking and want to try a variety of meals using just one appliance. In that case, an air fryer is just for you. So now you can ditch the junk food items and start preparing the crispy meal by adding just a tablespoon of oil.

This cookbook is best for beginners who want to learn about air fryers and how to cook a meal in them. However, this cookbook serves beyond that, as it is also for those who want to maintain a healthy lifestyle by consuming less fatty food.

It's been noticed that in today's fast pace society, everyone looks for ease and indulges in junk foods. Which in turn makes them obese, leading to several other health issues.

The air fried food is one of the healthiest among other conventional methods. The air fryer is also energy efficient as it consumes 80 % less energy than other appliances and prepares less fatty food. Writing this cookbook aims to provide all people with some authentic air fryer recipes that offer hand free cooking experience.

If you are a professional cook or a housewife, you can take advantage of this appliance, as the recipes introduced in this book are tasty and versatile. In addition, each recipe incorporated beautiful images of the final product to give the reader a glimpse of the final product and how it's been cooked. The recipes introduced in this cookbook are for homemakers or beginners and for someone who wants to lose weight. The air fryer helps you prepare less fussy meals.

This cookbook categorizes recipes: breakfast, quick and easy meals, chicken, turkey, beef, lamb, shrimp, seafood, dessert, snack, bread, vegetable, and pizza.

If you buy an air fryer to take advantage of all its benefits, choose the one that fits your budget and family needs. There are numerous air fryers in the market with different sizes, budgets, and functions. What works for someone does not work for others.

We hope that after grabbing this book, you will have an excellent idea of how to prepare meals in the air fryer. It's recommended not to over-panic with the temperature and time as, in the beginning, it's pretty hard to get settled with the appliance.

One should always have a clear idea of what will be prepared in the air fryer. Precise and effective shopping is needed to save money and time. The timing is a crucial factor as well. If you, as a beginner, follow a set of protocols, it significantly affects your overall health and budget.

Now you can develop a healthy relationship with your favorite food like pizzas, burgers, fries, and pancakes, as all of our recipes fit the budget and taste great.

The air fryer is way healthier than frying in oil. With very little to no oil used in the process, it cuts 70% to 80% of calories. So, frying in an air fryer and reducing oil intake promotes weight loss.

Our dilemma at the current time is that we love homemade food, but we don't have time to cook. Air fryer provides you with an opportunity for fast, safe, and easy cooking.

When you can prepare your chicken breast or chops in just 20 to 30 minutes, it's pretty sure that you will not order it from outside. If you are a crunch lover and prefer fried food because it's crispy and crunchy, then you should go for an air fryer. It turns your frozen and breaded food into a crispy exterior with a little cooking spray. You can reheat your leftover pizza slices and get the same fresh, crispy crust, thoroughly heated from inside.

The air fryer doesn't only provide you with a healthier alternative to deep frying; it is versatile as well. You can prepare various foods, from French fries, spring rolls, and fried chicken to curries and desserts.

Before starting the cooking process, it is essential to know what an air fryer is, its associated effort, and how to clean and maintain it.

Let gets to the next part of this cookbook.

What Is an Air Fryer?

Fried food has always attracted the taste bud of any individual. But this changing world has put us in a state where we need not be only conscious about the choice of food but also how it is cooked. The air fryer has made this task easy as it provides the taste and texture of deep-fried food but eliminates all the extra fat and calories that can harm your health.

An air fryer is a modern countertop appliance that can replace your deep fryers and oven and gives you a healthy substitute for your fried items. It works by circulating hot air around the food. As a result, it penetrates your food, makes it crunchy and crispy, and satisfies your appetite for fried items in a healthy way. Most air fryers require food to be misted with cooking spray or a teaspoon of oil to improve the texture and increase crispiness.

Benefits of the Air fryer

The air fryer craze is gaining popularity daily as more people buy it and realize its usefulness. There are several benefits of using an air fryer:

- The appliance offers easy maintenance. The air fryer cleaning is easy.

- It offers hand free cooking experience. It offers odor free cooking experience.

- The operation and function buttons are easy to operate. Air fryers have user friends displays

- It's a safe dishwasher appliance. It makes better-tasting food.

- It helps you to eat healthily in a delicious way. It did not burn the nutrients of the food.

- You can satisfy your food craving without adding extra pounds. It doesn't heat the surrounding environment.

- It handles frozen meals like a pro chef.

5 Tips for the Air fryer

Here are the top tips to get the best out of your air fryers.

- Always preheat your air fryer for 2 to 3 minutes before adding food. It saves your cooking time, and meals are ready faster than conventional cooking.

- Air fryer bottoms get very sticky after cooking, so layering them with parchment paper before cooking is advisable. It would collect all the grease without making a mess.

- Don't overfill your air fryer. Always leave space for the air to circulate properly in the food basket. Your food would not be crispy and brown evenly if the basket is overcrowded.

- Flip foods over halfway or as required by the recipe. One of the best parts of the air fryer is that you can open it as often as needed without interrupting your cooking time. Just take out the basket, flip your food, and insert it back in its place; you can shake the basket if you make French fries or nuggets.

- You can add a small amount of oil during the cooking process to make your food extra crispy, but be careful while adding that oil. Also, always spray your food outside the machine because spraying inside can cause a sticky buildup on the inner surface.

How to Clean the Air Fryer

Cleaning your air fryer is very important for its maintenance; you need a thorough cleaning after each use and a deep clean after every few uses.

- Unplug your air fryer after use and let it cool.

- Take out its basket, pan, tray, and other removable accessories. Wash all the parts thoroughly with warm soapy water.

- You can also put them in the dishwasher if the company's user manual instructs.

- Clean the exterior of the air fryer with a damp cloth to remove any fat traces inside the fryer.

- Dry all the parts; you can let them dry overnight.

- Wash the other main parts of your air fryer for proper functioning. Clean the heating coils with a damp towel.

Breakfast Recipes

Hard Boiled Eggs with Spinach and Tomatoes

Prep Time: 15 Minutes

Cook Time: 20 Minutes

Yield: 2 Servings

Ingredients

- 4 large organic eggs
- 1 cup baby spinach
- Salt and black pepper to taste
- 4 tablespoons of tomatoes, chopped
- 6 tablespoons of mayonnaise
- 1 teaspoon of paprika

Directions

1. Before starting the cooking process, preheat your air fryer to 355 degrees F for minutes. First, take a cooking pot and boil water in it.

2. Let the spinach leaves thawed in it for a few minutes. Then drain the spinach and set it aside.

3. Now chop the spinach leaves and add them to a bowl Let it sit to get cool.

4. Take out the air fryer basket from the unit. Then add the eggs to it.

5. Close the unit.

6. Set the timer to 15-16 minutes.

7. Set temperate to 250 degrees F.

8. Once the cooking time is complete, remove the eggs from the air fryer basket. Peel the eggs after dumping them in the cold-water bath.

9. Cut the eggs lengthwise.

10. Mix the yolks into a bowl with spinach, salt, tomatoes, pepper, and mayonnaise. Fill the egg whites with this mixture.

11. Serve and enjoy with a sprinkle of paprika.

Lemon Strawberry Corn Muffins

Prep Time: 20 Minutes

Cook Time: 15 Minutes

Yield: 2 Servings

Ingredients

- ½ cup cornmeal
- ¼ cup plain flour
- ½ teaspoon Baking Powder
- 2 teaspoons baking soda
- Pinch of salt
- 1/2 cup brown sugar
- 1 teaspoon of lemon zest
- ¼ cup orange juice
- 4 tablespoons butter
- 2 small eggs
- ¼ cup buttermilk
- ½ cup fresh strawberry, chopped and the green part removed
- Oil spray for greasing

Directions

1. Mix cornmeal, sugar, flour, baking soda, and baking powder in a large bowl. Mix it well so the ingredient incorporates.

2. Then pour in the orange juice, lemon zest, and salt.

3. Whisk eggs in a small bowl and add buttermilk and melted butter Whisk it well, and then add it to the flour bowl.

4. Fold in chopped strawberries.

5. Put muffin cup liner into ramekins and divide the batter between the ramekins, leaving some space on top.

6. Place the ramekins according to capacity inside the air fryer basket. Close the unit.

7. Adjust the temperature to 370 degrees F. Adjust the time to 15 minutes.

8. Once muffins are done, serve and enjoy.

Delicious Air Fryer Pancake with Raspberry Topping

Prep Time: 15 Minutes

Cook Time: 16-18 Minutes

Yield: 2 Servings

Ingredients

- 2 tablespoons unsalted organic butter, melted
- 4 organic eggs
- ½ cup all-purpose flour
- ½ cup almond milk
- 1 teaspoon vanilla
- 1 ½ cup fresh raspberry
- 2-4 tablespoons of
- Maple syrup for drizzling
- Oil spray for greasing

Directions

1. Before starting the cooking process, preheat your air fryer at 360 degrees F for a few minutes. Next, whisk eggs in a bowl.

2. Then add the butter, vanilla extract, and milk. Whisk it well, and then shift flour into the mixture.

3. Make a smooth batter.

4. Take a round pan that fits inside an air fryer basket. Mist the pan with oil spray.

5. Pour the batter into the pan.

6. Add the pan to the basket and close the unit. Cook for 16-18 minutes, until puffy.

7. Top the pancake with raspberries and drizzle maple syrup on top.

Breakfast Soufflé

Prep Time: 15 Minutes

Cook Time: 20-25 Minutes

Yield: 2 Servings

Ingredients

- ¼ cup all-purpose flour
- 1/3 cup butter
- 1 cup milk
- ¼ cup brown sugar
- Oil spray for greasing
- 4 egg yolks
- 1 teaspoon vanilla extracts
- 6 egg whites
- 1 ounce of white sugar
- 1 teaspoon of cream of tartar

Directions

1. Before starting the cooking process, preheat your air fryer to 400 degrees F for a few minutes.

2. Put the flour and butter into a bowl and mix with your hands. Take a small saucepan and heat milk along with sugar.

3. Once the sugar melts, bring the milk to a boil.

4. Add the flour to the mixture at this stage and stir vigorously so no lump forms. Simmer it for 5 minutes until the mix thickens.

5. Remove it from heat and let it cool for 15 minutes. Next, oil greases the soufflé dishes with oil spray. In a bowl, whisk egg yolks and vanilla extract.

6. Add in the flour milk mixture and mix it well.

7. In a medium bowl, beat egg whites, white sugar, and cream of tartar. Fold this into the soufflé base and pour the prepared flour mixture on top. Put it in the air fryer basket.

8. Close the unit.

9. Set the time to 15 minutes.

10. Adjust the temperature to 320 degrees F. Once done, serve.

French toast

Prep Time: 15 Minutes

Cook Time: 5 Minutes

Yield: 2 Servings

Ingredients

- 1 organic eggs
- 2 tablespoons of almond milk
- 1 teaspoon vanilla extract
- ¼ teaspoon of cinnamon
- 2 large and thick slices of bread
- 2 tablespoons Butter for spreading
- 1/3 cup maple syrup for drizzling

Directions

1. Before starting the cooking process, preheat your Air fryer to 400 degrees F. Take a bowl and crack eggs in it.

2. Pour the milk with butter and vanilla extract, and whisk it well.

3. Add a pinch of cinnamon as well.

4. Now soak the bread slices into the batter. Line an air fryer basket with parchment paper Put the bread slices onto the air fryer basket. Add it to the unit and close the lid.

5. Adjust the time to 3-5 minutes.

6. Adjust the temperature to 360 degrees F.

7. Flip the bread slices halfway through cooking.

8. Once it's done, serve with the drizzle of maple syrup.

Air Fryer Banana Bread

Prep Time: 15 Minutes

Cook Time: 10 Minutes

Yield: 2 Servings

Ingredients

- 1 1/3 cups of flour
- 1/2 cup of milk
- 1 teaspoon of baking powder
- 1 teaspoon of baking soda
- 1 teaspoon of cinnamon
- 1 teaspoon of salt
- 2/3 cups of sugar
- 1/2 cup of oil
- 4 overripe bananas, peeled and mashed

Other:
- Oil spray for greasing

Directions

1. Take a large mixing bowl and attach the mixing paddles to it. Dump in the flour and milk and turn the speed to medium.

2. Then add all the remaining listed ingredients one by one. Now take a loaf pan and grease it with oil spray.

3. Pour the banana bread batter into it.

4. Add the loaf pan into the air fryer and close the unit. Adjust the time to 330 degrees F

5. Adjust the temperature to 20 minutes.

6. If the toothpick comes out clean when inserted in the middle of the bread, it's ready. If it's not done yet, cook for 10 more minutes.

7. Once cool, slice and serve.

Mushroom Omelet in Air Fryer

Prep Time: 15 Minutes

Cook Time: 6-8 Minutes

Yield: 2 Servings

Ingredients

- 4 eggs, whisked
- 2 tablespoons of butter
- 1/3 cup almond milk
- ½ cup cheese, grated
- Salt and pepper to taste
- 1 small onion
- 2 mushrooms, chopped

Directions

1. Before starting the cooking process, preheat your air fryer to 355 degrees F. Whisk eggs in a bowl.

2. Then pour in milk and butter.

3. Whisk it well and add grated cheese, salt, and black pepper. Then add the chopped onions and mushrooms, and mix well. Pour the egg mixture into oil-greased ramekins.

4. Add the ramekins to the air fryer and close the unit. Adjust the time to 6-8 minutes.

5. Adjust the temperature to 350 degrees F. Once done, serve.

Toad-In-The-Hole

Prep Time: 15 Minutes

Cook Time: 10 Minutes

Yield: 2 Servings

Ingredients

- 1 large sheet of frozen puff pastry, thawed
- 4 tablespoons Parmesan cheese, shredded
- 4 tablespoons diced spam
- 4 eggs, organic
- 4 tablespoons heavy cream
- 4 red tomatoes slices

Directions

1. Before starting the cooking process, preheat your air fryer to 390 degrees F for a few minutes. Unfold the pastry sheet onto a clean and flat surface.

2. Then cut the sheet into equal squares.

3. Layer the sheet onto the basket or rack and cook for 5 minutes. Take it out once puffed.

4. Create an indentation by pressing with a spoon in the middle. Now layer each indication with spam and one egg on top.

5. Sprinkle cheese at the end with tomato slices.

6. Put it back into the air fryer and air fry for 5-7 minutes. Work in batches and cook all the remaining squares.

7. Serve with a garnish of heavy cream. Enjoy.

Breakfast Frittata

Prep Time: 15 Minutes

Cook Time: 18 Minutes

Yield: 3 Servings

Ingredients

- 1/3-pound sausage, cooked and crumbled
- 6 small eggs, lightly beaten
- ½ cup cheddar cheese, shredded
- 4 tablespoons green bell pepper, chopped
- ½ green onion, chopped
- Pinch of salt
- Pinch of black Pepper
- Oil spray for greasing

Directions

1. Before starting the cooking process, preheat your air fryer to 370 degrees F for 4-6 minutes. Whisk eggs in the bowl.

2. Then add the sausage, cheese, green bell pepper, onions, salt, and black pepper. Mix everything well.

3. Grease a cake pan with oil spray. Pour the prepared mixture into it.

4. Add the cake pan to the air fryer and close the unit. Adjust the time to 18 minutes.

5. Adjust the temperate to 360 degrees F. Once done, serve.

Breakfast Tortilla Wraps

Prep Time: 15 Minutes

Cook Time: 13-15 Minutes

Yield: 4 Servings

Ingredients

- 8 eggs, whisked
- ½ avocado, chopped
- 1 cup of mozzarella cheese, grated
- Salt and pepper to taste
- 4 tortillas wrap
- ½ cup tomatoes, chopped

Directions

1. Before starting the cooking process, preheat your air fryer to 360 degrees F for 4-6 minutes. Whisk eggs in a medium bowl and season it with salt and pepper.

2. Take a shallow tin and grease it with oil spray. Pour the egg into the tin.

3. Put the tin in the air fryer and close the unit Adjust the time to 8 minutes.

4. Afterward, take out the eggs and fill the tortilla with eggs, cheese, tomatoes, and avocado. Wrap it up and add it to the air fryer basket or rack lined with aluminum foil.

5. Air fries it for 5 minutes. Once done, serve.

Quick Easy Recipes

Bacon-Wrapped Potato Tots

Prep Time: 15 Minutes

Cook Time: 10 Minutes

Yield: 2 Servings

Ingredients

- 10 potato tots, extra crispy
- 10 bacon strips, sliced medium
- 4 tablespoons sour cream
- Oil spray for greasing

Directions

1. Wrap each potato tot with one bacon strip. Repeat for all the tots.

2. Arrange it onto an oil-greased air fryer basket or a rack. Close the unit.

3. Adjust the temperate to 400 degrees F Adjust the time to 10 minutes.

4. Once the timer is complete, take the tots and serve them with cream cheese.

Mozzarella Sticks

Prep Time: 15 Minutes

Cook Time: 7-10 Minutes

Yield: 3 Servings

Ingredients

- 1.5 pounds block of mozzarella cheese
- ½ cup of all-purpose flour
- 2 eggs, whisked
- 2 tablespoons almond milk
- 1 cup Panko breadcrumbs
- 4 ounces tomato ketchup

Directions

1. Before starting the cooking process, preheat your air fryer to 390 degrees F for 2-4 minutes. Cut the cheese into sticks about 4-inch.
2. Take a bowl and dredge the flour into it.
3. In a separate bowl, whisk eggs with milk.
4. Take another bowl and add Panko bread crumbs to it.
5. Dip the cheese sticks into flour, then in eggs wash, and then in the Panko bread crumbs. Grease an air fryer basket with oil spray or line it with parchment paper.
6. Add the basket to the air fryer. Close the unit.
7. Adjust the temperature to 390 degrees F.
8. Adjust the time to 7-10 minutes, flipping halfway through.

9. Once all the sticks are ready, serve with ketchup or any other sauce of your liking.

Garlic Coated Potato Wedges In Air Fryer

Prep Time: 20 Minutes

Cook Time: 12 Minutes

Yield: 2 Servings

Ingredients

- 4 medium potatoes, unpeeled, cut into wedges (1-inch chunks)
- 1 teaspoon of chopped cilantro
- ¼ teaspoon of lemon zest
- 1 tablespoon of corn flour
- 1 teaspoon of garlic, minced
- Salt and black pepper to taste
- ¼ teaspoon of rosemary
- Oil spray for misting

Directions

1. Fill a large bowl with ice-filled cold water and soak the potato wedges for 40 minutes.

2. Boil the wedges in boiling water for 3 minutes and then drain and pat dry the wedges with a paper towel.

3. Next, mix rosemary, pepper, cilantro, lemon zest, corn flour, and salt in a bowl. Mix well and toss the wedges in it.

4. Mist the wedges with oil spray.

5. Then add the wedges to an air fryer basket lined with parchment paper Add the basket to the unit.

6. Close the unit.

7. Adjust time to 12 minutes

8. Adjust the temperate to 400 degrees F. Shake the basket halfway through.

9. Once done, serve and enjoy.

Garlic Knots

Prep Time: 12 Minutes

Cook Time: 10 Minutes

Yield: 2 Servings

Ingredients

- 12 ounces of pizza dough
- Salt and black pepper to taste
- 4 tablespoons of olive oil
- 1/3 cup parmesan cheese
- 3 garlic cloves, minced
- 1 cup marinara sauce

Directions

1. Before starting the cooking process, preheat your air fryer to 395 degrees F. Lay the pizza dough on a flat, clean surface

2. Cut the dough lengthwise into strips

3. Roll the strips between the palms of the hands and make medium-sized knots or round shapes. Combine salt, garlic, pepper, cheese, and olive oil.

4. Brush the knot shapes with the bowl mixture.

5. Add it to an air fryer basket lined with parchment paper. Add the basket to the air fryer.

6. Close the unit.

7. Adjust time to 10 minutes

8. Adjust the temperate to 375 degrees F. Flip the garlic knots halfway through.

9. Once done, serve and enjoy with marinara sauce.

Spinach and Cheese Muffins

Prep Time: 20 Minutes

Cook Time: 15-20 Minutes

Yield: 2 Servings

Ingredients

- 4 strips of breakfast bacon, chopped
- ½ purple onion, chopped
- ½ cups cheddar cheese, shredded
- 1/4 cup of spinach
- 4 large organic eggs
- Salt and black pepper to taste

Directions

1. Take a skillet and cook bacon strips in it until crispy. Take out the strip and set it aside on the paper towel Now in the same skillet, cook onion in bacon fat.

2. Next, put the spinach and cook for 2 minutes.

3. Now take ramekins and divide the bacon strip on the bottom of the ramekins. Top it with the cooked spinach and onion mix.

4. Crack one egg on top of each ramekin and season it with salt and pepper. Add cheddar cheese on top of ramekins.

5. Put it in the air fryer basket. Add the basket to the air fryer. Close the unit.

6. Adjust the time to 12 minutes. Adjust the template to 375 degrees F. Once done, serve.

Artichokes with Honey Dijon

Prep Time: 20 Minutes

Cook Time: 12-15 Minutes

Yield: 2 Servings

Ingredients

- 4 whole artichokes
- 10 cups of water
- Sea salt, to taste
- ½ cup raw honey
- ¼ cup boiling water
- 4 tablespoons of Dijon mustard
- A handful of cilantro, chopped

Directions

1. Remove the outer leaves of the artichokes. Then cut the tips.
2. Cut the artichokes in half, lengthwise.
3. Turn the artichokes so the cut side is facing you.
4. Fill a pot with water and add a few pinches of salt to it. Mix it and add the artichokes.
5. Let the artichokes sit in it for 15-25 minutes. Then drain and set aside/
6. Take a bowl and combine Dijon mustard, cilantro, honey, and water Mix it well
7. Brush the artichokes with this sauce.
8. Place the artichokes into an air fryer basket lend with parchment paper. Insert the basket into the air fryer and close the unit.

9. Adjust the time to 12-15 minutes Adjust the temperate o 350 degrees F Once it's done, serve.

Simple Jicama Chip

Prep Time: 14 Minutes

Cook Time: 12 Minutes

Yield: 2 Servings

Ingredients

- 10 ounces jicama, cut into small sticks after peeling
- 1& 1/2 tablespoon avocado or olive oil
- 1/2 tablespoon paprika
- 1/2 tablespoon garlic powder
- 1/2 tablespoon salt
- Pinch of cayenne Pepper
- Few drops of lime

1. **Directions**
2. Put the jicama chips into a large bowl and add all the remaining listed ingredients. Toss well for fine coating.
3. Grease an air fryer basket with oil spray.
4. Place it onto the air fryer basket in a single layer. Close the unit.
5. Adjust the temperate to 400 degrees F Adjust the time to 12 minutes.
6. Toss or flap the jicama sticks halfway through. Serve with your favorite dipping sauce.

Stuffed Jalapeno Peppers

Prep Time: 10 Minutes

Cook Time: 14 Minutes

Yield: 2 Servings

Ingredients

- 1 cup cream cheese
- 6 jalapeno peppers, sliced lengthwise
- 1 cup Panko bread crumbs
- oil spray for greasing

Directions

1. Wash the jalapeno pepper and pat dry with a paper towel. Cut the pepper lengthwise and discard the seeds.

2. Fill the cavity of the peppers with cream cheese.

3. Coat it with Panko bread crumbs and mist it with oil spray. Put it in the air fryer and close the unit.

4. Adjust the time to 14 minutes. Adjust the temperate t 360 degrees F.

5. Once done, serve.

Crispy Chicken Fingers with Ranch Dressing

Prep Time: 15 Minutes

Cook Time: 12 Minutes

Yield: 4 Servings

Ingredients

- 2 pounds of chicken breast fillet, cut into strips
- Salt and black pepper to taste
- 2 tablespoons olive oil
- 3 eggs, whisked
- 2 ounces of ranch dressing seasoning mix
- 2 cups bread crumbs

Directions

1. Cut the chicken breast into strips or finger shapes. Season it with salt, pepper, and ranch dressing.

2. Toss it well for fine coating.

3. Whisk eggs in a bowl.

4. In a separate bowl, add Panko bread crumbs.

5. Dump the strip into egg wash, then in Panko bread crumbs. Coat the strips well.

6. Place it on an air fryer basket or rack lined with parchment paper. Close the unit.

7. Adjust the time to 12 minutes

8. Adjust the temperature to 390 degrees F. Remember to flip the finger strips halfway. Once done, serve.

Quick Pita Pizza

Prep Time: 15 Minutes

Cook Time: 5 Minutes

Yield: 1 Serving

Ingredients

- 1 pita bread
- 1-2 tablespoons tomato sauce
- ¼ cup mozzarella cheese, shredded
- 1 tablespoon of extra virgin oil
- cup basil leaves

Directions

1. Before starting the cooking process, preheat your air fryer to 400 degrees F for a few minutes. Take pita bread and spread a generous amount of tomato sauce on it.

2. Top it with cheese and add a splash of olive oil.

3. Add it to the air fryer and close the unit Adjust the time to 5 minutes.

4. Once it's done, serve with a topping of basil leaves.

Chicken Recipes

Glazed Chicken Breast with Basil Corn Salad

Prep Time: 15 Minutes

Cook Time: 12 Minutes

Yield: 4 Servings

Ingredients

Ingredients for Marinade:

- ¼ cup olive oil
- 1 garlic cloves, minced
- ½ cup white wine vinegar
- 1/2 cup soy sauce, reduced-sodium
- ¼ cup Worcestershire sauce
- 1 teaspoon lemon juice
- Salt and black pepper to taste
- 2 tablespoons of Italian seasoning
- 2 teaspoons of smoked paprika
- 4 tablespoons of mustard
- ½ cup maple syrup

Chicken Ingredient:

- Oil spray for greasing 8 chicken breasts

Salad ingredients:

- 2 cups fresh corn
- 1 cup cherry tomatoes, halved
- 1cup crumbled feta
- 1/4 red onion, finely chopped
- ½ cup basil, thinly sliced
- 1 tablespoons of extra-virgin olive oil
- Juice of 1 lime
- Salt and black pepper to taste

Directions

1. Before starting the cooking process, preheat your air fryer to 350 degrees F for a few minutes. Mix all the marinade ingredients in a bowl.

2. Add chicken breasts to the marinade and coat the chicken well. Let the chicken sit in the marinade for 2 hours in the refrigerator. In a large separate bowl, toss all the salad ingredients together.

3. Place the salad bowl in the refrigerator to keep it fresh.

4. Now layer the chicken breast pieces on to air fryer basket or rack lined with parchment paper. Work in batches or according to the capacity of the air fryer.

5. Close the unit and adjust the time to 22 minutes Adjust temperate to 370 Degrees F.

6. Remember to flip the chicken halfway through.

7. Once done, take out the chicken and serve it with prepared salad.

Chicken Tenders With Potato Salad

Prep Time: 25 Minutes

Cook Time: 12 Minutes

Yield: 4 Servings

Ingredients

Chicken Ingredients

- 2 pounds of chicken tender or drumsticks
- 2 tablespoons of sachet McCormick kits crumb seasoning
- Oil spray for greasing
- 1/2 cup Japanese-style mayonnaise
- 2 teaspoons of pickled ginger, reserved
- 2 tsp pickling liquid

Potato Salad Ingredients

- 1 pound russet potatoes, cooked chopped
- Salt, to taste
- 2 teaspoons of apple cider vinegar
- 1 cup mayonnaise
- ¼ cup celery, ⅛-inch dice
- 1/3 cup sweet pickle relish
- 4 tablespoons red onions, ⅛-inch dice
- 4 tablespoons minced parsley
- 2 teaspoons Dijon mustard
- 1/4 teaspoon onion powder

Directions

1. Before starting the cooking process, preheat your air fryer to 400 degrees F for 5 minutes. Combine all the salad ingredients in a bowl, mix well and add it to the refrigerator for chilling and keeping it fresh.

2. Meanwhile, coat the chicken with all the listed ingredients under the chicken. Let it sit for 30 minutes.

3. Next, add the chicken to the air fryer basket lined with parchment paper. Add the basket to the unit.

4. Close the air fryer.

5. Set time to 10-12 minutes

6. Set temperature to 370 degrees F. Flip the tenderloins halfway through.

7. Once done, take the chicken tenderloin and serve with prepared potato salad.

BBQ Chicken With Baked Potatoes

Prep Time: 25 Minutes

Cook Time: 22 Minutes

Yield: 4 Servings

Ingredients

- 4 pounds of chicken breast, boneless, skinless
- ½ teaspoon paprika
- ½ teaspoon garlic powder
- Salt and cracked black pepper to taste
- ⅓ - ½ cayenne peppers optional
- Oil spray for greasing
- 2/3 cup BBQ sauce

Directions

1. Add paprika, garlic powder, pepper, salt, and cayenne to a bowl. Coat the breast pieces with the prepared rub.

2. Grease the pieces with oil spray.

3. Grease an air fryer basket with oil spray or line it with parchment paper. Layer the breast piece onto the chicken.

4. Set the temperate to 370 degrees F. Set the timer to 22 minutes.

5. Flip the chicken halfway through.

6. Then take out the chicken and brush it with BBQ sauce

7. Put the chicken back into the air fryer and air fry it for 3 more minutes. Take it out; let it get cool for 5 minutes

8. Then serve

Pistachio Crusted Chicken

Prep Time: 22 Minutes

Cook Time: 12 Minutes

Yield: 2 Servings

Ingredients

- 2(6 ounces each) chicken breast, boneless, skinless
- Salt and black pepper to taste
- 4 tablespoons of mayonnaise
- ½ cup roasted pistachios, crushed
- Oil spray for greasing

Directions

1. Season the chicken breast pieces with salt and black pepper. Then coat it with mayonnaise.

2. Add the pistachios to a bowl and coat all the chicken breast pieces to make a delicate crust.

3. Add the chicken to an air fryer basket lined with parchment paper Add the basket to an air fryer

4. Close the unit.

5. Set timer to 12 minutes

6. Adjust the temperate to 380 degrees F, flipping halfway through Once it's cooked, serve and enjoy.

Cosmic Wings

Prep Time: 20 Minutes

Cook Time: 15-20 Minutes

Yield: 4 Servings

Ingredients

- 2 pounds of chicken wings
- 1 tablespoon garlic powder
- ½ tablespoon onion powder
- ½ tablespoon paprika
- 1 tablespoon dried parsley
- 1/4 teaspoon salt
- 1/3 teaspoon of rosemary
- 1/4 teaspoon pepper
- 8 ounces Cosmic Jerry Sauce
- 1 lemon, juice only

Directions

1. Combine onion powder, garlic powder, salt, pepper, paprika, parsley, and rosemary in a bowl.

2. Coat the wings with this dry rub Mist the wings with oil spray.

3. Layer the wing son to oil greased basket and air fryer the wings in the air fryer. Adjust the time to 15-20 minutes.

4. Adjust the temperate to 360 degrees F, flipping halfway through. Once wings are done, toss them with the cosmic jerry sauce.

5. Serve and enjoy with a drizzle of lemon juice on top.

Air Fryer Chicken Parmesan Meatballs With Pasta

Prep Time: 30 Minutes

Cook Time: 15 Minutes

Yield: 2 Servings

Ingredients

- 1 & 1/2 pounds of ground chicken breast
- 1 cup Panko breadcrumbs
- 2 small eggs
- 1 tablespoon Italian seasoning
- Salt and black pepper to taste
- ½ cup parmesan cheese
- ½ cup marinara sauce
- 1/3 cup shredded mozzarella cheese
- 2 cups pasta, personal choice
- Oil spray for misting

Directions

1. Combine salt, pepper, parmesan cheese, breadcrumbs, ground chicken, eggs, and Italian seasoning in a bowl and mix it well so the ingredients incorporate. Make meatballs of the mixture.

2. Mist the meatballs with oil spray.

3. Add the meatballs to the air fryer basket lined with parchment paper. Close the unit.

4. Adjust the item to 12-15 minutes.

5. Meanwhile, cook the pasta according to package instructions. Adjust the temperate to 370 degrees.

6. Remember to flip the meatballs halfway through cooking. Now take out the chicken and top it over marinara sauce. Serve them over cooked pasta with a sprinkle of cheese.

BBQ Chicken Breasts With Coleslaw

Prep Time: 25 Minutes

Cook Time: 25 Minutes

Yield: 4 Servings

Ingredients

- 4 chicken breasts, frozen boneless, skinless (8 ounces each)
- 2 tablespoons olive oil
- Salt and black pepper to taste
- 1 cup of barbecue sauce
- 1 cup coleslaw, homemade

Directions

1. Before starting the cooking process, preheat your air fryer to 400 degrees F for 5 minutes. Thaw the frozen chicken before cooking.

2. Rub the chicken with salt, pepper, and olive oil.

3. Add the chicken to an oil-greased basket of air fryers. Add the basket to the unit, and close the unit.

4. Adjust the time to 22-25 minutes Adjust the temperate to 370 degrees F Remember to flip the breasts halfway.

5. Baste the chicken every 5 minutes with BBQ sauce.

6. Once done, serve and enjoy with coleslaw and the remaining sauce. Enjoy hot.

Chicken Tomatina With Rice

Prep Time: 15-20 Minutes

Cook Time: 22 Minutes

Yield: 2-4 Servings

Ingredients

- 4 chicken breasts, boneless and skinless
- ¼ cup fresh basil leaves
- ½ cup Parsley
- 8 plum tomatoes
- 3/4 cup lemon juice
- 2 tablespoons olive oil
- 1 teaspoon of ginger garlic paste
- Salt and black pepper to taste
- 2 tablespoons of coconut aminos
- 2 cups of cooked or steamed rice

Directions

1. Take a high-speed blender and add parsley, basil, olive oil, ginger garlic paste, salt, lemon juice, black pepper, and coconut amino.

2. Pulse it into a paste.

3. Then add tomatoes and pulse them into a smooth paste.

4. Transfer this paste or sauce to a bowl and add the chicken breasts. Marinate the chicken in the refrigerator for 60 minutes.

5. Take out the chicken and add the marinade chicken along with the marinade in a round pan. Add this pan to the air fryer basket or rack.

6. Close the unit

7. Set timer to 22 minutes

8. Set temperate to 370 degrees F.

9. Once the chicken is tender, take it and serve over cooked rice with the sauce collected at the bottom of the round pan.

10. Enjoy hot.

Roasted Cinnamon Apple With The Chicken

Prep Time: 15 Minutes

Cook Time: 22-25 Minutes

Yield: 2 Servings

Ingredients

- 2 gala apples, peeled and sliced round
- 4 tablespoons organic butter
- 1 tablespoon orange zest
- 1/3 teaspoon cinnamon
- 1 pound of whole chicken, pieces, or cut in half
- Salt and black pepper to taste
- 1 teaspoon of garlic powder
- Oil spray for greasing

Directions

1. Before starting the cooking process, preheat your air fryer to 370 degrees F. Grease an air fryer basket with oil spray or line it with parchment paper.

2. Arrange apples on the air fryer basket and sprinkle cinnamon on top. In a bowl, mix butter with orange zest.

3. Rub the chicken with garlic powder, salt, and black pepper Rub the butter mix all over the chicken.

4. Add the chicken on top of the apples. Add the basket to the unit and close it. Adjust the timer to 22-25 minutes Adjust the tie to 370 degrees F

5. Once done, serve

Crispy Fillets With Sriracha Honey Sauce

Prep Time: 25 Minutes

Cook Time: 20-22 Minutes

Yield: 2 Servings

Ingredients

Chicken Sauce

- 1/3 cup mayonnaise
- 3 tablespoons raw honey
- 6 tablespoons Sriracha sauce or to taste

Chicken Batter Ingredients

- ½ cup buttermilk
- ½ cup all-purpose flour, more if needed
- ½ cup cornstarch
- 2 eggs, whisked
- 2 teaspoons Sriracha sauce or to taste
- Salt and black pepper to taste

Other Ingredients

- 1 pound of chicken breast cut in half
- 2 cups Panko bread crumbs
- Oil spray for greasing

Directions

1. Take a large bowl and combine all the chicken batter ingredients. Mix well and set aside for further use.

2. Mix all the chicken sauce ingredients in a second bowl and whisk well. Arrange the Panko bread crumbs on a baking sheet.

3. Coat the chicken with the batter mixture, then coat it with the Panko breadcrumbs. Repeat this step for all the pieces.

4. Arrange it on an air fryer basket lined with parchment paper. Add the basket to the unit.

5. Close the unit.

6. Adjust the time to 20-22 minutes

7. Adjust the temperature to 370 degrees F. Flip the breast pieces halfway.

8. Once done, serve with prepared sauce. Enjoy.

Turkey Recipes

Turkey Croquettes

Prep Time: 22 Minutes

Cook Time: 12-14 Minutes

Yield: 4 Servings

Ingredients

- 1 cup smashed potatoes
- 1/2 cup grated Parmesan cheese
- 1/2 cup shredded Swiss cheese
- 1 finely chopped shallot
- 2 teaspoons minced fresh rosemary
- 1 teaspoon minced fresh sage
- Salt and black pepper to taste
- 3 cups finely chopped cooked turkey
- 1 large egg
- 2 tablespoons water
- 1-1/4 cups Panko bread crumbs
- Butter-flavored cooking spray

Ingredients for Cranberry Dip:

- 1 cup cranberry sauce
- ½ cup sour cream
- 1 tablespoon horseradish
- ¼ teaspoon of black Pepper
- 2 jalapenos, seeded and diced

Directions

1. Before starting the cooking process, preheat your air fryer to 400 degrees F for 5 minutes. Meanwhile, mix mashed potatoes, shallots, sage, salt, pepper, rosemary, and both kinds of cheese in a bowl.

2. Add the turkey meat and mix well.

3. Make patties and mist the patties with oil spray. Whisk eggs in a bowl.

4. Put the Panko bread crumbs in another bowl.

5. Dip patties in egg wash, then coat them with bread crumbs. Arrange patties in the air-fryer basket lined with parchment paper. Cook for 12-14 minutes, flipping halfway through.

6. Meanwhile, prepare the sauce; combine all the cranberry dip in a bowl. Mix and serve with Turkey Croquettes.

7. Enjoy.

Turkey Sandwich Melt

Prep Time: 15 Minutes

Cook Time: 7-8 Minutes

Yield: 2 Servings

Ingredients

- 2 ciabatta rolls
- 4 tablespoons mayonnaise
- 6-8 slices of peppered turkey
- 4 slices of mild cheddar cheese
- 4 slices of cooked bacon, cut in half
- 1 sliced thinly Roma tomato
- 1 ripe avocado
- 8-10 pepperoncini peppers
- ½ cup of spring mix lettuce
- 4-6 tablespoons of mustard

Directions

1. Before starting the cooking process, preheat your air fryer to 400 degrees F for 5 minutes. Slice the ciabatta roll into slices and spread the mayonnaise onto the pieces.

2. Toast the slices in the air fryer at 400 degrees F for 3 minutes, mayonnaise side facing up. Then take it out of the air fryer.

3. Now divide the cheese into slices, turkey meat slices, and pre-cooked bacon. Place the slices back into the air fryer.

4. Air fry for 4 minutes at 400 degrees F

5. Remove the slices and assemble the sandwiches by layer the avocado, pepperoncini, tomatoes, spring mix lettuce or sprouts, and personally preferred sauces like mustard.

6. Cut the sandwiches and serve.

Air Fryer Turkey Breast

Prep Time: 20 Minutes

Cook Time: 40 Minutes

Yield: 2 Servings

Ingredients

- 2 pounds turkey breast, on the bone with skin
- 1 tablespoon olive oil
- Salt, to taste
- 1 tablespoon dry turkey seasoning

Directions

1. Before starting the cooking process, preheat your air fryer to 350 degrees F for a few minutes. Coat the turkey breast with olive oil
2. Season the turkey breasts with salt and dry turkey seasoning.
3. Line a basket of air fryers with parchment paper. Add the turkey breast to it
4. Add it to the air fryer and close the unit. Adjust the temperature to 350 degrees F. Adjust the time to 22 minutes
5. Flip the breasts halfway.
6. The internal temperature should be 160 degrees F. It needs 18 more minutes of cooking.
7. Once done, serve.

Air Fryer Garlic Herb Turkey Breast

Prep Time: 15 Minutes

Cook Time: 40 Minutes

Yield: 4 Servings

Ingredients

- 1pounds turkey breast, skin on
- Salt Black Pepper to taste
- 4 tablespoons butter, melted
- 4 cloves garlic, minced
- ½ teaspoon freshly chopped thyme
- 1teaspoon freshly chopped rosemary
- 1 teaspoon of sage

Directions

1. Pat dries the breasts and season them with salt and pepper.
2. Combine melted butter, thyme, sage, garlic, and rosemary in a bowl and brush it over the turkey breast.
3. Place the breasts in the air fryer basket lined with parchment paper
4. Mist the breast with oil spray. Close the unit
5. Adjust the temperate to 370 degrees F
6. Adjust the time to 40 minutes, flipping halfway through Once done, serve after letting it cool.

Juicy Air Fryer Turkey

Prep Time: 25 Minutes

Cook Time: 40-50 Minutes

Yield: 4 Servings

Ingredients

- 4-pound bone-in turkey breasts
- 4 tablespoons olive oil
- 1tablespoons Italian seasoning
- 2 teaspoon paprika
- ½ teaspoon garlic powder
- Salt and black pepper to taste
- 4 tablespoons butter

Directions

1. Coat the turkey breasts with olive oil.

2. Season it with salt, Pepper, Italian seasoning, paprika, and garlic powder. Put butter slices under the skin of the turkey.

3. Lay the turkey skin side down onto the air fryer basket lined with parchment paper. Air fry the turkey at 350 degrees for 20 minutes, flipping halfway

4. It may need additional air frying for 25-30 minutes

5. In the end, the internal temperate should be 165 degrees F.

6. Remove the turkey from the basket and let rest for 15 minutes before slicing and serving.

Beef Recipe

Beef Tenderloin

Prep Time: 25 Minutes

Cook Time: 22-25minutes

Yield: 2 Servings

Ingredients

- 2 tablespoons of olive oil
- 1 pound of beef back rib
- 1/ 4 cup cherries, peeled
- 1 large onion, peeled
- ¼ cup of brown sugar
- ¼ teaspoon of paprika
- 1tablespoon of pork rubs seasoning
- Salt and black pepper to taste

Directions

1. Take a bowl and whisk oil with brown sugar, salt, black pepper, paprika, and pork rub seasoning. Coat the 2 pounds of beef back rib with the marinade.

2. Let it sit for 1 hour for marinating.

3. Take an air fryer basket and grease it with oil spray.

4. Add 2 pounds of beef back rib, onions, and cherries surrounding the rib. Add the basket to the unit.

5. Close the unit

6. Adjust the time to 22-25 minutes

7. Adjust the temperature to 3 60 degrees F. Flip the beef back rib halfway through.

8. Let it air fryer a little more if you want it to be more cooked. It should give a medium rare beef.

9. Once done, serve and enjoy.

Pear Bake Tri-Tip Steaks

Prep Time: 25 Minutes

Cook Time: 12-15 Minutes

Yield: 1-2 Servings

Ingredients

- 1 Tri-Tip Steaks
- 2 garlic cloves, minced
- ½ teaspoon ground cumin
- ½ teaspoon dried oregano
- 1/4 cup lime juice
- 2 tablespoons olive oil

Pear Salad

- 2 jalapeno peppers, seeded and chopped
- 2 tablespoon lime juice
- 2 pears, chopped peeled
- 4 teaspoons sugar
- ½ cup chopped red onion
- ½ tablespoon chopped mint
- ½ tablespoon lime zest, grated
- Salt and black pepper to taste

Directions

1. Rub the Tri Tip Steaks with listed spices and oil. Let it sit for 20 minutes before cooking.

2. Take a large bowl and add all the listed pear ingredients. Put the Tri Tip Steaks into the air fryer.

3. Adjust the time to 12-15 minutes

4. Adjust the temperatures to 400 degrees F. Flip the chops halfway.

5. Serve the tenderloin with a prepared pear salad.

Beef Milanese with Stuffed Mushrooms

Prep Time: 25 Minutes

Cook Time: 35 Minutes

Yield: 2 Servings

Ingredients

- 2 eggs, beaten
- 2 cups seasoned breadcrumbs
- 4 beef chops, thin-sliced boneless
- 6-ounce cream cheese
- 1/2 cup sour cream
- 1 cup baby spinach, thawed
- ¼ teaspoon Garlic powder
- Salt and black pepper to taste
- 5 medium-sized Portobello mushrooms, cored
- 1 cup Parmesan cheese, shredded

Directions

1. Before starting the cooking process, preheat your air fryer to 400 degrees F for a few minutes. Season the pork chops with salt and black pepper.

2. Add the Panko bread crumbs to a tray. Whisk the eggs in a small bowl.

3. Dump the pork chops in the eggs and wash them in the Panko bread crumbs. Take an air fryer basket or rack and line it with parchment paper.

4. Add the chop init

5. Add it to the unit and close the unit Adjust the time to 25 minutes

6. Adjust the temperature to 360 degrees F. Flip the chops halfway.

7. meanwhile, in a bowl, mix sour cream, garlic powder, spinach, salt, pepper, and cream cheese along with parmesan cheese

8. Fill the mushroom cavity with it

9. Take out the pork chops once done and add mushrooms to the air fryer Air fry for 14-15 minutes at 375 degrees F

10. Serve the chops with stuffed mushrooms. Enjoy.

Juicy Vegetables And Sirloin Steak With Sour Cream

Prep Time: 25 Minutes

Cook Time: 20 Minutes

Yield: 2 Servings

Ingredients

- 1.5 pounds beef sirloin steak, cut into strips
- ½ cup diced tomatoes, undrained
- 6 ounces green beans, halved
- 5ounces of frozen pearl onions, thawed
- 1 tablespoon paprika
- 1 cup sour cream
- Oil spray for greasing
- Salt and black pepper to taste
- 1 cup salsa
- 2-4 tortilla wraps, warm

Directions

1. Before starting the cooking process, preheat your air fryer to 400 degrees F for 5 minutes. In a bowl, add steak bites, green beans, onions, and tomatoes,

2. Season all of it with salt, pepper, and paprika.

3. Transfer the ingredients to an air fryer basket lined with parchment paper. Add the basket to the Inuit.

4. Close the unit.

5. Air fryer it for 20 minutes at 370 degrees F, flipping the ingredients halfway.

6. Take the ingredients and serve over tortilla wrap with a dollop of sour cream and salsa.

Beef Stuffed Bell Peppers

Prep Time: 25 Minutes

Cook Time: 20 Minutes

Yield: 2 Servings

Ingredients

- 1.5 pounds beef sirloin steak, cut into strips
- ½ cup diced tomatoes, un-drained
- 6 ounces green beans, halved
- 6 ounces of frozen pearl onions, thawed
- 1 tablespoon paprika
- 1 cup sour cream
- Oil spray for greasing
- Salt and black pepper to taste
- 1 cup salsa
- 2-4 tortilla wraps, warm

Directions

1. Before starting the cooking process, preheat your air fryer to 400 degrees F for 5 minutes. In a bowl, add steak bites, green beans, onions, and tomatoes,

2. Season all of it with salt, pepper, and paprika.

3. Transfer the ingredients to an air fryer basket lined with parchment paper. Add the basket to the Inuit.

4. Close the unit.

5. Air fryer it for 20 minutes at 370 degrees F, flipping the ingredients halfway.

6. Take the ingredients and serve over tortilla wrap with a dollop of sour cream and salsa.

Sticky Sweet Beef Ribs with Baked Potatoes

Prep Time: 30 Minutes

Cook Time: 45-50 Minutes

Yield: 2 Servings

Ingredients

- 6 short ribs
- 2 teaspoons minced garlic
- 2 tablespoons olive oil
- 2 tablespoons brown sugar
- 2 tablespoons oyster sauce
- Salt, to taste
- 1 teaspoon sesame oil

Side Servings:

- 2 baking potatoes, large
- Sauce Ingredients:
- 1/2 cup lemon juice
- 1/2 cup honey
- 4tablespoons reduced-sodium soy sauce
- 2 garlic cloves, minced

Directions

1. Before starting the cooking process, preheat your air fryer to 400 degrees F for 4 minutes. Add ribs, garlic, oil, brown sugar, oyster sauce, salt, and sesame oil in a bowl.

2. Coat the ribs well.

3. Add the ribs to an air fryer basket. Adjust the time to 16 minutes.

4. Adjust the temperatures to 400 degrees F.

5. Meanwhile, bake potatoes in the oven at 400 degrees F for 30-40 minutes.

6. Mix all the sauce ingredients in a bowl. Once done, arrange all the ingredients on a plate and serve with sauce drizzle.

Air Fryer Rib Eye

Prep Time: 25 Minutes

Cook Time: 16-18 Minutes

Yield: 2 Servings

Ingredients

- 6 tablespoons of Greek yogurt
- 4 tablespoons of fresh cream
- ¼ teaspoon of cumin powder
- 1 tablespoon of coriander seeds, crushed
- 1/2 teaspoon paprika
- 1 teaspoon Italian seasoning
- 4 tablespoons lemon juice
- Salt and black pepper to taste
- 2 rib-eye steaks, 16 ounces each

Directions

1. Combine Greek yogurt, cream, salt, and pepper in a bowl. Mix well and add all the listed spices and lemon juice.

2. Coat the beef ribs with marinade and refrigerate for 20 minutes.

3. Next, remove it from the refrigerator and add it to the air fryer basket lined with parchment paper.

4. Adjust the time to 16-18 minutes and the temperature to 400 degrees F. Flip the beef ribs halfway through.

5. Once cooked, serve.

Maple Glazed Rib Eye Steak

Prep Time: 25 Minutes

Cook Time: 16-18 Minutes

Yield: 2 Servings

Ingredients

- Salt and black pepper to taste
- 1.5 pounds rib eye
- 1/4 tablespoon garlic, minced
- 2 tablespoons of olive oil
- 1 tablespoon lemon juice
- ½ teaspoon of thyme
- ½ tablespoon fresh rosemary, chopped
- ½ cup Maple syrup

Directions

1. Before starting the cooking process, preheat your air fryer to 400 degrees F for 5 minutes. Coat the rib eye with lemon juice, salt, pepper, thyme, garlic, rosemary, and olive oil.

2. Add the steak to the air fryer basket lined with parchment paper Close the unit.

3. Air fries it at 400 degrees F for 16-18 minutes, flipping halfway through. Baste the steak with maple syrup every 8 minutes during cooking.

4. Once done, serve.

Chipotle New York Steak

Prep Time: 22 Minutes

Cook Time: 16-18 Minutes

Yield: 2 Servings

Ingredients

- 1 New York steaks, 16 ounces each
- 1 tablespoon chipotle powder
- 1 tablespoon dark brown sugar
- 1/3 teaspoon cumin
- Oil spray for greasing
- 2 tablespoons of olive oil

Directions

1. Before starting the cooking process, preheat your air fryer to 400 degrees F for a few minutes. Rub the steak with oil, brown sugar, chipotle powder, salt, and cumin and set it aside for a few minutes.

2. Then grease an air fryer basket with oil spray or line it with parchment paper. Add the steak onto the air fryer basket

3. Add the basket to unit Close the unit

4. Adjust the time to 16-18 minutes

5. Adjust the temperatures to 400 degrees F Remember to flip halfway through.

6. Once done, serve, and enjoy.

Marinated Beef Roast

Prep Time: 30 Minutes

Cook Time: 55 Minutes

Yield: 3 Servings

Ingredients

- 1.5 pounds of Beef roast

Marinade Ingredients

- 1/3 cup white wine
- 1/2 tablespoon balsamic vinegar
- 2 tablespoons rosemary, fresh

Stuffing Ingredients

- 1/3 cup onion, caramelized
- 1/3 cup spinach, frozen
- 1/2 tablespoon black pepper, freshly ground

Directions

1. Combine all the listed marinade ingredients in a bowl Mix all the stuffing ingredients in a separate bowl.
2. Layer the beef on a clean flat surface.
3. Put the stuffing in the middle and roll the meat Secure it with twine.
4. Brush the beef with the marinade and let it sit for 30 minutes in the refrigerator Add it to the air fryer basket.
5. Adjust the time to 55 minutes.
6. Adjust the temperatures to 400 degrees F

7. Take it out once done; allow it to rest for 10 minutes before slicing and serving.

Lamb Recipes

Herbed and Garlic Lamb Rack

Prep Time: 20 Minutes

Cook Time: 14 Minutes

Yield: 2 Servings

Ingredients

- 2 pounds of a rack of lamb
- 4 tablespoons of olive oil
- 2 teaspoons of rosemary
- 2 teaspoons of thyme
- ½ teaspoon of garlic powder
- Salt and black pepper to taste

Directions

1. Before starting the cooking process, preheat your air fryer to 390 degrees F for a few minutes. Pat Dry the lamb rack with a paper towel.

2. Remove any silver skin from the rack of lamb. Cut it into individual chops.

3. Add oil, rosemary, thyme, garlic powder, salt, and black pepper to a bowl. Toss the lamb chops in this marinade.

4. Let it sit in refrigerators for a few hours. Grease an air fryer basket with oil spray.

5. Place lamb chops in a single layer into an air fryer basket. Adjust the time to 14 minutes

6. Adjust the temperature to 380 degrees F. Flip halfway.

7. Then serve.

Raspberry Chipotle Lamb Chop

Prep Time: 20 Minutes

Cook Time: 14-16 Minutes

Yield: 2 Servings

Ingredients

- 8 lamb chops
- 2 cups of homemade coleslaw
- 1 cup cheese sauce

Sauce Ingredients

- 4 teaspoons of chipotle seasoning
- 1/4 cup coconut amino
- ½ cup raspberry sauce
- 4 tablespoons honey
- ½ teaspoon garlic powder
- Salt, to taste
- 1/4 teaspoon of paprika powder

Directions

1. Combine all the sauce ingredients in a bowl and whisk well.
2. Marinate the chops in the sauce for 1 hour by placing them in the refrigerator. Add it to an air fryer basket lined with parchment paper.
3. Close the unit.
4. Adjust the time to 14-16 minutes.
5. Adjust the temperature to 400 degrees, flipping halfway through. Meanwhile, take a small saucepan and add leftover marinated sauce to it. Mix it with cheese sauce once cool.
6. Cook for a few minutes until simmer.

7. Once it's done, serve hot with coleslaw and cheese sauce.

Mustard Lamb Chops With Chimichurri Sauce

Prep Time: 12 Minutes

Cook Time: 14 Minutes

Yield: 2 Servings

Ingredients

- 1 1/2 pounds of lamb chops
- 4 teaspoons of olive oil
- 1/2 cup Parmesan cheese grated
- 1 teaspoon onion powder
- 2 teaspoons mustard powder
- Salt and black pepper to taste
- 1 teaspoon of paprika powder
- 1 teaspoon of garlic powder

Chimichurri Sauce Ingredients:

- 1 shallot, chopped
- 1 red jalapeño, chopped
- garlic cloves, chopped
- ½ cup red wine vinegar
- Salt, to taste
- ½ cup cilantro, chopped
- ¼ parsley, chopped
- 2 teaspoons of oregano, chopped
- ½ cup extra-virgin olive oil

Directions

1. Take a bowl and add all the sauce ingredients and whisk well Then set aside for further serving.

2. Take a large bowl and add oil, salt, onion powder, mustard powder, pepper, paprika, and garlic powder.

3. Coat the chops with this spice mixture.

4. Add it to an air fryer basket lined with parchment paper Add it to the unit and adjust the time to 14 minutes Adjust the temperature to 350 degrees F.

5. Let it air fry, flipping halfway through. Once it's done, serve and enjoy with sauce.

Bourbon Lamb Chops With Baked Potatoes

Prep Time: 25 Minutes

Cook Time: 14-16 Minutes

Yield: 2 Servings

Ingredients

Ingredients for marinade:

- ½ tablespoon dry mustard powder
- 3 tablespoons brown sugar, packed
- 1/3 cup bourbon
- 2 tablespoons Worcestershire sauce
- 2 tablespoons soy sauce
- ½ cup balsamic vinegar
- Salt and black pepper to taste
- 8 pork chops

Salad Ingredients:

- 6 red tomatoes, chopped
- 2 cucumbers, peeled, deseeded, roughly chopped
- 1 red onion thinly sliced
- 12 Kalamata olives
- ¼ teaspoon of dried oregano
- 1 cup of feta cheese, cut into chunks
- 6 teaspoons of olive oil

Directions

1. Combine all the salad ingredients in a bowl and toss well. Mix all the marinade ingredients in a bowl.

2. Marinate the chops for 1 hour by placing them in the refrigerator. Then add the chop to the air fryer basket lined with parchment paper. Add it to a fryer and close the unit.

3. Adjust the time to 14-16 minutes. Adjust the temperature to 400 degrees F. Flip the chops halfway through.

4. Once done, serve with baked potatoes.

Sticky Sweet Lamb Ribs

Prep Time: 15 Minutes

Cook Time: 25 Minutes

Yield: 2 Servings

Ingredients

- 8 lamb ribs
- 2 teaspoon minced garlic
- 2 tablespoons olive oil
- 3 tablespoons brown sugar
- 3 tablespoons oyster sauce
- Salt, to taste

Directions

1. Before starting the cooking process, preheat your air fryer to 400 degrees F for 8 minutes. Take a large bowl and add lamb ribs.

2. Add garlic, olive oil, brown sugar, oyster sauce, and salt to a bowl and mix well. Line a parchment paper onto a basket of the air fryer.

3. Lay the chops on it according to capacity.

4. Add it to the unit. Close the unit.

5. Adjust the temperature to 360 degrees F.

6. Adjust the time to 25 minutes, flipping halfway. Once done, serve.

Fish Recipes

Steamed Salmon With Lemon And Herbs

Prep Time: 20 Minutes

Cook Time: 10-12 Minutes

Yield: 2 Servings

Ingredients

- 2 onions (sliced)
- 2spring onion (sliced lengthwise)
- 1.5 pounds salmon filet (skin on, 4 portions)
- Salt and black pepper to taste
- 1 teaspoon coriander, grounded
- 1 teaspoon cumin, grounded
- 1 teaspoon Aleppo pepper
- 2 cloves garlic (chopped)
- 4 tablespoons of extra virgin olive oil
- 2 tablespoons of partly
- 1 lemon, sliced
- ¼ cup white wine vinegar

Directions

1. Before starting the cooking process, preheat your air fryer to 400 degrees F for a few minutes. Line a tray with aluminum foil.

2. Slice or chop the onions and add them on top of aluminum foil.

3. Now take a bowl and add salt, olive oil, black Pepper, Aleppo pepper, coriander, white wine vinegar, cumin, salt, and pepper.

4. Rub this spice mixture all over the salmon.

5. Now put salmon on top of the onion, salmon, and skin side down. Top it with garlic, green onions, and parsley.

6. Add the lemon slices to the side of the salmon. Now foil packs the salmon and secures the corners. Cover it and add it to the air fryer basket.

7. Adjust the time to 10-12 minutes. Adjust the temperature to 380 degrees F

8. Once done, unwrap the foil and serve with all prepared ingredients.

Halibut with Vegetables

Prep Time: 20 Minutes

Cook Time: 8-10 Minutes

Yield: 2 Servings

Ingredients *Sauce Ingredients* 2 Lemons zest

- 1 lemon, juice only
- 1 cup extra virgin olive oil
- 1 ½ tablespoon garlic, minced
- 2 teaspoon dill
- 1 teaspoon seasoned salt
- ½ teaspoon black pepper
- 1 teaspoon dried oregano
- ½ teaspoon coriander

For The Fish

- 1 pound of green beans
- 1 onion (sliced to half-moon)
- 1½ pound halibut (cut into 1-inch pieces)

Side Servings

- 2 cups cooked jasmine rice
- 1 cup salsa

Directions

1. Before starting the cooking process, preheat your air fryer to 400 degrees F for a few minutes. Combine all the sauce ingredients in a bowl and marinate the ingredients for fish in it for 30 minutes.

2. Then line an aluminum foil in a double layer inside an air fryer basket Add fish, green beans, and onions on aluminum foil in an air fryer basket. Foil pack the ingredients

3. Add it to the air fryer and close the unit. Adjust the time to 8-10 minutes.

4. Flip the fish and veggies halfway through. Adjust the temperatures to 400 degrees F.

5. Meanwhile, put rice, coconut milk, and water in a rice cooker. Cook the rice according to manual instructions.

6. Serve the fish over cooked jasmine rice Top it with salsa.

Pecan Sauce with Salmon

Prep Time: 25 Minutes

Cook Time: 20 Minutes

Yield: 2 Servings

Ingredients

- 2 salmon fillets, 6 ounces each
- Salt and black pepper to taste
- ½ cup maple syrup

Sauce Ingredients

- ½ Orange Rosemary Sauce
- 1/4 cup orange juice
- 4 rosemary sprigs
- ½ cup pecans, chopped
- 2 tablespoons brown sugar

Additional Ingredients

- 6 tablespoons unsalted butter
- 3 tablespoons all-purpose flour

Directions

1. Coat the salmon with maple syrup, salt, and pepper.
2. Then add it to an air fryer basket lined with aluminum foil. Add it to the unit and top the salmon with pecans.
3. Close the unit.
4. Adjust the time to 12 minutes.
5. Adjust the temperatures to 380 degrees F.

6. Meanwhile, prepare the sauce by combining all the sauce ingredients in a saucepan and letting it cook at low for 5-8 minutes until simmering.

7. Next, combine butter and flour and add them to a sauce. Cook just until thickened.

8. Once the salmon is cooked, drizzle the prepared sauce over the top and enjoy hot.

Mahi Fillets With Mango Salsa

Prep Time: 20 Minutes

Cook Time: 12 Minutes

Yield: 2 Servings

Ingredients

Sauce Ingredients

- ½ cup sweetened coconut milk
- 1/4 cup Soy sauce
- 3 teaspoons Lemon juice
- ½ teaspoon red pepper flakes
- ½ teaspoon ginger

Other Ingredients

- 4-6 Mahi steaks, 6 ounces each

Ingredients for Mango Salsa

- 3 mangoes, peeled and chopped
- 1 Red bell pepper, chopped
- ½ small red onion, chopped
- 2 jalapenos, chopped
- ¼ cup cilantro
- 2 tablespoons Extra Virgin Olive Oil
- 1 lime, juice only
- Salt and black pepper to taste

Directions

1. Take a bowl and mix all the sauce ingredients in it.
2. Put the fish in the sauce and marinate it for 60 minutes.

3. Shake off excess liquid and place the fish onto the foil-filled air fryer basket. D adds it to the unit.

4. Close the unit.

5. Adjust the time to 400 degrees F for 12 minutes.

6. Meanwhile, add all the mango salsa ingredients to a medium bowl and serve air fry salmon.

Crispy Fish Fillets

Prep Time: 20 Minutes

Cook Time: 16 Minutes

Yield: 2 Servings

Ingredients

- 1 cup seasoned flour
- 2 eggs, organic
- ½ cup buttermilk
- 2 cups seafood fry mix
- ½ cup bread crumbs
- 2 codfish fillets, 4-6 ounces each
- Oil spray for greasing

Directions

1. Whisk eggs in a bowl and add buttermilk to it.

2. In a large bowl, combine seafood mix, seasoned flour, and Panko bread crumbs. Coat the fillet with eggs and then coat it with bread crumbs mixed.

3. Add the fish fillet to the air fryer basket lined with parchment paper. Add it to the unit.

4. Close the unit.

5. Adjust the time to 16 minutes

6. Adjust the temperatures to 380 degrees F. Flip the fillets halfway through

7. Once it's cooked, serve and enjoy.

Fish with Spicy Herb Vinaigrette

Prep Time: 20 Minutes

Cook Time: 12 Minutes

Yield: 2 Servings

Ingredients

Dressing /Dressing Ingredients

- ½ cup parsley leaves
- 1 cup basil leaves
- ½ cup mint leaves
- 2 tablespoons thyme leaves
- 1/4 teaspoon red pepper flakes
- 2 cloves of garlic
- 4 tablespoons of red wine vinegar
- ¼ cup of olive oil
- Salt, to taste

Other Ingredients

- 1.5 pounds of fish fillets, codfish
- 2 tablespoons olive oil
- Salt and black pepper to taste
- 1 teaspoon of paprika
- 1teaspoon of Italian seasoning

Directions

1. Add all the dressing ingredients to a bowl and whisk until smooth. Season the fish fillets with oil, salt, pepper, paprika, and Italian seasoning Add the fillets to an air fryer basket lined with parchment paper.

2. Add the basket to the unit. Close the unit.

3. Adjust the time to 12 minutes.

4. Adjust the temperature to 400 degrees F. Flip the fillet halfway through

5. Serve with the drizzle of prepared vinaigrette.

Cajun Salmon

Prep Time: 20 Minutes

Cook Time: 10-12 Minutes

Yield: 2 Servings

Ingredients

- 2 salmon fillets, 4 ounces each
- ½ tablespoon of Cajun seasoning
- ½ tablespoon of jerk seasoning
- 2 tablespoons of lemon juice
- Oil spray for greasing
- 1 cup blue cheese dressing

Directions

1. Combine the lemon juice, Cajun seasoning, and jerk seasoning in a bowl.
2. Set it aside for further use.
3. Now, grease an air fryer basket with oil spray.
4. Season the fillets with spice rub and mist them with oil spray. Now put the salmon fillets inside the air fryer basket.
5. Adjust the temperature to 390 degrees F. Adjust the time to 8-12 minutes.
6. Flip the salmon halfway through.
7. Once done, serve the fish fillets with blue cheese dressing.

Sweet Glazed Salmon

Prep Time: 20 Minutes

Cook Time: 10-12 Minutes

Yield: 2 Servings

Ingredients

- 1/3 cup maple syrup
- 1/4 cup sweet soy sauce
- 2 ounces orange juice
- 4 tablespoons Lemon juice
- ¼ tablespoon Red Wine Vinegar
- 4 teaspoons olive oil
- 4 cloves of garlic
- 2 scallions, chopped finely
- 3 salmon fillets, 4 ounces each
- Salt and ground black pepper to taste

Directions

1. Whisk maple syrup, garlic, soy sauce, orange juice, lemon juice, red wine vinegar, and salt in a bowl.

2. Add it to a saucepan and let it cook until thickened. Set it aside for further use.

3. Rub the salmon with salt, pepper, and olive oil. Line an air fryer basket with parchment paper.

4. Brush the salmon with the prepared sauce and add it to the basket. Adjust the timer to 10-12 minutes

5. Adjust the temperature to 400 degrees F. Baste the fish fillet every 5 minutes of cooking

6. Once done, serve it with chopped scallions and the remaining sauce.

Sundried Tomato with Salmon

Prep Time: 20 Minutes

Cook Time: 10-12 Minutes

Yield: 2 Servings

Ingredients

- 2 salmon fillets, 6 ounces each
- 1/3cup chopped fresh parsley
- 4 tablespoons Sun-Dried Tomato Dressing
- Oil spray
- Salt and black pepper to taste
- 4 Cherry tomatoes
- 1-1/2 cup broccoli

Directions

1. Before starting the cooking process, preheat your air fryer to 400 degrees F for 3 minutes. Add salt, pepper, sun-dried tomato dressing, cherry tomato, parsley, and broccoli into a bowl. Season the fish fillets with salt, pepper, and oil.

2. Rub it all over the fish

3. Now add the fish to the air fryer basket lined with parchment paper. Top it with veggies mix

4. Add it to the unit. Close the unit

5. Adjust the time to 12 minutes.

6. Adjust the temperature to 400 degrees F Flip the fillets and veggies halfway.

7. Once done, serve and enjoy.

Salmon with Green Pesto Sauce

Prep Time: 20 Minutes

Cook Time: 12 Minutes

Yield: 2 Servings

Ingredients

- 2 salmon fillets, 4 ounces each
- Salt and black Pepper
- 1 tablespoon of melted butter

Ingredients for Green Sauce

- 1 cup mayonnaise
- 1 teaspoon of pesto
- 6 tablespoons Greek yogurt
- Salt and black pepper to taste

Directions

1. Rub the salmon fillets with butter, salt, and black pepper.
2. Mix pesto, mayonnaise, Greek yogurt, salt, and black pepper in a small bowl. Add the fish fillet to the air fryer basket.
3. Close the unit.
4. Adjust the time to 12 minutes
5. Adjust the temperature to 400 degrees F. Flip the fish halfway through.
6. Serve with prepared pesto sauce.

Shrimp Recipes

Bacon-Wrapped Buffalo Shrimp

Prep Time: 20 Minutes

Cook Time: 12 Minutes

Yield: 1 Serving

Ingredients

- 10 shrimps
- 1 cup buffalo wing sauce
- 10 slice bacon
- ½ cup ranch

Directions

1. Take a large bowl and add the buffalo sauce and shrimp to it. Coat the shrimp well with the mixture.
2. Let it sit in the refrigerator for 1 hour.
3. Now wrap each shrimp with a bacon strip and add it to the air fryer basket lined with parchment paper.
4. Add it to the unit.
5. Adjust the time to 12 minutes.
6. Adjust the temperature to 390 degrees F. Flip the shrimp halfway.
7. Once done, serve with ranch.

Lemon Pepper Shrimp with Butter Sauce

Prep Time: 20 Minutes

Cook Time: 10-15 Minutes

Yield: 2 Servings

Ingredients

- 1 pound raw shrimp, peeled and deveined
- 1/3 cup olive oil
- 4 tablespoons lemon juice
- Salt and black pepper to taste

Sauce Ingredients

- ½ cup butter
- 4 cloves of garlic, minced
- Salt and pepper to taste
- 1 lemon juice
- 1 tablespoon chopped parsley

Directions

1. Cook the pasta according to package instructions. Preheat your air fryer to 400 degrees F for 5 minutes.

2. Add shrimp, salt, olive oil, lemon juice, and black pepper to a bowl.

3. Layer parchment paper onto an air fryer rack or basket and add shrimp to it. Add the basket to the unit.

4. Adjust the time to 10 minutes

5. Adjust the temperature to 390 degrees F.

6. Melt butter in a microwave and then add the remaining sauce ingredients Mix well and serve it with cooked shrimp.

7. Once it's done, serve.

Easy Popcorn Shrimp

Prep Time: 12 Minutes

Cook Time: 10 Minutes

Yield: 1 Serving

Ingredients

- 6-8 ounces popcorn shrimp, frozen
- Oil spray for greasing
- 1 cup coleslaw, homemade and fresh

Directions

1. Before starting the cooking process, preheat your air fryer to 400 degrees F for a few minutes. Add the frozen popcorn shrimps to oil greased air fryer basket

2. Adjust the time to 10 minutes

3. Adjust the temperature to 390 degrees F Flipping and shaking halfway through. Once done, serve with coleslaw.

Shrimp, Mushroom, and Broccoli

Prep Time: 10 Minutes

Cook Time: 10 Minutes

Yield: 1- 2 Servings

Ingredients

- 1 pound of shrimp
- 2 garlic cloves, minced
- ½ cup broccoli
- 2 tablespoons of soy sauce
- 1 teaspoon of brown sugar
- Oil spray for greasing
- 1 tablespoon of lemon juice
- ½ pound of shitake mushroom

Directions

1. Combine the shrimp, soy sauce, garlic, broccoli, brown sugar, mushrooms, and lemon juice in a bowl and toss well.

2. Take a small baking pan and grease it with oil spray.

3. Add the bowl ingredients to an oil-greased air fryer basket. Add the basket opt the jut

4. Close the unit

5. Adjust the time to 10 minutes

6. Adjust the temperature to 390 degrees F. Shake the basket halfway through.

7. Once it's done, serve and enjoy.

Simple Shrimp

Prep Time: 15 Minutes

Cook Time: 12 Minutes

Yield: 1 Serving

Ingredients

- 10 large shrimp, raw, peeled, & deveined
- 1 cup unsweetened coconut, dried
- 1 cup Panko breadcrumbs
- 2 large eggs
- 1 tablespoon Cornstarch
- 1 cup flour

Directions

1. Before starting the cooking process, preheat your air fryer for 5 minutes at 320 degrees F. Add the shrimp to a paper towel and pat dry it after washing and cleaning.

2. Combine the coconut flakes and breadcrumbs onto a baking sheet, and set it aside for further use. Whisk eggs in a bowl.

3. Combine the flour with corn starch in a separate tray.

4. Dump the shrimps in the flour mixture, wash the eggs, and finally, into the coconut mixture. Layer it onto a parchment paper-lined air fryer basket.

5. Add the basket to the unit Adjust the time to 12 minutes

6. Adjust the temperature to 320 degrees F Flip the shrimp halfway.

7. Once done, serve and enjoy.

Pizza Recipes

Crab Pizza

Prep Time: 15 Minutes

Cook Time: 10-12 Minutes

Yield: 2 Servings

Ingredients

- 1 tablespoon butter
- 1-3/4 cups sliced fresh mushrooms
- 2 small onions, chopped
- 2 small sweet red peppers cut into strips
- 2 garlic cloves, minced
- Salt and black pepper to taste
- 1-1/4 cups imitation crabmeat (about 1/2 pound), coarsely chopped
- 8-inch pizza crust, premade
- Oil spray for greasing
- 1/2 cup Alfredo sauce
- ½ cup mozzarella cheese

Directions

1. Take a cooking pan and melt butter in it.

2. Then sauté onion s and mushrooms and season it with salt, pepper, and garlic. Add the crab to it and cook for 2 minutes.

3. Preheat your air fryer to 400 degrees F for 5 minutes

4. Then layer a pizza crust onto an air fryer basket lined with parchment paper. Pre-cook it for 3 minutes.

5. Take the basket out.

6. Top the crust with Alfredo sauce and cooked crab meat mixture. Spread it evenly.

7. Sprinkle cheese on top. Now add it to the air fryer
8. Adjust the time to 8-10 minutes.
9. Adjust the temperature to 375 degrees F. Close the door.
10. Cook until done, serve, and enjoy.

Chicken Pizza

Prep Time: 15 Minutes

Cook Time: 10 Minutes

Yield: 2 Servings

Ingredients

- 1 (8-inch) pizza crust, prebaked

Toppings

- 1 pound chicken breasts, boneless skinless and cut into 1-inch strips
- 2 tablespoons olive oil
- 1/2 cup prepared pesto
- 4 cherry tomatoes, halved
- 1 small onion, sliced
- 4 tablespoons of olives
- 1//3 cup mushrooms, sliced
- 1 cup mozzarella cheese

Directions

1. Before starting the cooking process, preheat your air fryer to 400 degrees F for 2 minutes. Heat oil in a skillet and cook chicken pieces for 15 minutes, until tender and brown

2. Set it aside.

3. Now place the pizza crust in an air fryer basket lined with parchment paper and greasy with oil spray.

4. Precook the crust for 2 minutes Spread pesto evenly onto the crust

5. Then top it with cooked chicken, tomatoes, olives, mushrooms, onions, and cheese. Add it to the air fryer.

6. Adjust the time to 8 minutes

7. Adjust the temperature to 400 degrees F Close the door.

8. Once done, serve.

Cheese and Broccoli Pizza

Prep Time: 15 Minutes

Cook Time: 10-12 Minutes

Yield: 2 Servings

Ingredients

- 8 ounces store-bought pizza base
- Oil spray for greasing

Toppings Ingredients

- ½ cup cream cheese
- ½ cup mayonnaise
- 1 teaspoon of dry ranch dressing
- 1 cup broccoli cut into small chunks
- ½ cup bell pepper, sliced
- ¼ cup of red bell peppers
- ½ cup corn, canned and drained
- 1/3 cup olives, sliced
- 1 cup cheese, personal choice

Directions

1. Before starting the cooking process, preheat your air fryer to 400 degrees F for 2 minutes. Combine the dry ranch dressing with cream cheese and mayonnaise, then set aside.

2. Mist the air fryer basket with oil spray.

3. Place the pizza crust onto the oil-greased basket and pre-cook for 3 minutes. Then top it with cheese mix, broccoli, olives, and bell pepper

4. S and top it with cheese mixes.

5. Then add to the cauliflower, broccoli, corn, and red bell pepper. Add the end and add cheese.

6. Add it to the air fryer.

7. Adjust the time to 8-10 minutes

8. Adjust the temperature to 375 degrees F Close the door.

9. Once done, serve.

Eggplant Pizza

Prep Time: 15 Minutes

Cook Time: 10 Minutes

Yield: 2 Servings

Ingredients

- 8-inches store-bought thin-crust pizza dough
- ½ cup pizza sauce

Toppings Ingredients

- 1 medium Japanese eggplant, sliced and peeled
- ¼ teaspoon of oregano
- 1/4 teaspoon of thyme
- 1/3 cup thinly sliced mushrooms
- 2 small red onions
- ½ yellow bell pepper, sliced
- 6 ounces shredded mozzarella cheese

Directions

1. Before starting the cooking process, preheat your air fryer to 400 degrees F for 2 minutes. Grease an air fryer basket with oil spray.

2. Lay the pizza dough in the basket and pre-cook for just 2 minutes. Take out the crust and layer it with pizza sauce.

3. Add the listed toppings one by one, sprinkling cheese at the end Add it back opt the air fryer.

4. Adjust the time to 8 minutes.

5. Adjust the temperature to 400 degrees F Once it's done, serve.

All Cheese Pizza

Prep Time: 15 Minutes

Cook Time: 10-12 Minutes

Yield: 2 Servings

Ingredients
- 8 inches thin-crust pizza dough
- Oil spray for greasing

Topping Ingredients
- ¼ cup of mayonnaise
- 1/3 cup ricotta cheese
- 3 slices of fresh mozzarella
- 3 cloves of garlic
- 1 teaspoon red pepper flakes

Directions

1. Preheat your air fryer to 400 degrees F for 2 minutes. Grease an air fryer basket with oil spray.

2. Put the pizza crust in an oil-greased basket. Precook for 3 minutes

3. Take it out and spread mayonnaise all over.

4. Then add the listed toppings one by one, spreading evenly. Sprinkle the cheese at the end.

5. Add it back to the air fryer. Adjust the time to 8 minutes.

6. Adjust the temperature to 400 degrees F Once it is done, serve.

Snacks And Bread

Air Fried Tofu

Prep Time: 15 Minutes

Cook Time: 15 Minutes

Yield: 2-3 Servings

Ingredients

- 1.5 pounds of tofu, drained and cut into cubes
- 4 organic eggs
- 6 tablespoons nonfat milk
- ½ cup of almond flour
- 1 cup of breadcrumbs

Toppings:

- Sesame seeds, as needed

Directions

1. Cut the tofu block into 2 inches slices.

2. Mix breadcrumbs with almond flour in a bowl and set aside.

3. Whisk milk and eggs in a large bowl and dredge tofu cubes in the egg wash and flour. Add it to an air fryer basket lined with parchment paper.

4. Adjust the time to 12 minutes

5. Adjust the temperature to 390 degrees F. Flip the cubes halfway through

6. Once it's done, top with sesame seeds.

Potato Wedges

Prep Time: 15 Minutes

Cook Time: 22 Minutes

Yield: 2 Servings

Ingredients

- 4 sweet potatoes cut into wedges
- 2 teaspoons of olive oil
- Salt and black pepper
- Paprika, to taste

Directions

1. Slice the potato wedges in the cold water and let them sit for about 2 hours. Take it out from the water and pat dry with a paper towel.

2. Season it with salt, paprika, olive oil, and black pepper. Coat it well.

3. Add it to the air fryer basket lined with parchment paper. Adjusts the time to 20-22 minutes.

4. Adjust the temperature to 400 degrees F. Once it's done, serve.

Onion Rings

Prep Time: 5 Minutes

Cook Time: 12-16 Minutes

Yield: 2 Servings

Ingredients

- 12 ounces of frozen battered onion rings

Directions

1. Put the onion rings into the frying basket. Cook at 320 degrees F for 12-16 minutes. Serve.

Air-Fried Apple Chips

Prep Time: 15 Minutes

Cook Time: 16 Minutes

Yield: 2 Servings

Ingredients

- 4-6 apples, peeled, cored, and thinly cut
- 1/2 teaspoon of ground cinnamon
- 4 tablespoons sugar
- Pinch of sea salt to taste

Directions

1. Use a mandolin cutter to slice the apples thinly. Preheat your air fryer to 390 degrees F.

2. Put the apple slices on a baking sheet. Grease it with oil spray.

3. In a bowl and, add sugar, salt, cinnamon. Drizzle it over the apple slices.

4. Add the apples to the air fryer basket, lined with parchment paper. Add it to the unit.

5. Adjust the time to 16 minutes

6. Adjust the temperature to 300 degrees F. Serve and enjoy.

Kale Chips

Prep Time: 10 Minutes

Cook Time: 5 Minutes

Yield: 2 Servings

Ingredients

- 2 cups of kale, stems, and ribs removed
- 4 tablespoons of olive oil
- Salt and black pepper to taste

Directions

1. Before starting the cooking process, preheat your air fryer to 390 degrees F. Combine kale, olive oil, salt, and black pepper in a bowl.

2. Toss it well.

3. Layer it onto an air fryer basket lined with parchment paper. Adjust the time to 5 minutes

4. Adjust the temperature to 400 degrees F. Once it's done, serve.

5. Enjoy.

Vegetable Recipes

Purple Medley

Prep Time: 12 Minutes

Cook Time: 20 Minutes

Yield: 2 Servings

Ingredients

- 2 beets, chopped
- 2 purple carrots, chopped
- ½ cup red onion, chopped
- 2 tablespoons balsamic vinegar
- Salt and black pepper to taste

Directions

1. Before starting the cooking process, preheat your air fryer to 400 degrees F for 10 minutes. Add beets, carrots, red onion, balsamic vinegar, salt, and black pepper to a bowl.

2. Mix it well and add it to the air fryer basket lined with parchment paper.

3. Add the basket to the unit.

4. Insert the basket into the air fryer and close the unit. Adjust the time to 20 minutes.

5. Adjust the temperatures to 400 degrees F. Once done, serve and enjoy.

Simple Jicama Chip

Prep Time: 10 Minutes

Cook Time: 12 Minutes

Yield: 1 Serving

Ingredients

- 2-3 jicamas cut into sticks
- 1/2 tablespoon avocado or olive oil
- 1/2 tablespoon paprika
- 1/4 tablespoon garlic powder
- Salt and black pepper to taste
- 2 tablespoons of lime juice

Directions

1. Wash and cut the jicama into thin sticks

2. Add the sticks to a medium bowl and coat them with the remaining ingredients. Add it to an air fryer basket lined with parchment paper.

3. Adjust the time to 12 minutes

4. Adjust the temperature to 400 degrees F Shake the basket halfway through

5. Once it's done, serve and enjoy with your favorite dipping sauce. Enjoy.

Easy Ratatouille

Prep Time: 12 Minutes

Cook Time: 10 Minutes

Yield: 2 Servings

Ingredients

- 1 medium eggplant
- 1 medium zucchini
- 1 medium red tomato
- 1 yellow bell pepper
- 1 red bell pepper
- 1 medium-sized onion
- 1 fresh cayenne pepper, chopped
- 6 sprigs of fresh basil, diced
- 4 sprigs of fresh oregano, chopped
- 4 clove garlic (crushed)
- Salt and black pepper to taste
- 2 tablespoons olive oil
- 2 tablespoons white wine
- 2 teaspoons vinegar

Directions

1. Before starting the cooking process, preheat an air fryer to 400 degrees F for a few minutes. Add all the sliced and chopped vegetables to a bowl and all the remaining listed ingredients. Toss well to coat

2. Pour it into the air fryer basket greased with oil spray. Close the unit.

3. Adjust the time to 10 minutes

4. Adjust the temperature to 400 degrees F, flipping halfway through. Once done, serve.

Air Fryer Vegetable Nuggets

Prep Time: 14 Minutes

Cook Time: 10 Minutes

Yield: 4 Servings

Ingredients

- 4 Potatoes mashed after boiling
- 1 cup cooked Peas, crushed
- 1 cup broccoli grated
- 1 cup Soy nuggets (soaked and crushed)
- 1 cup Bread crumbs
- 5 tablespoons Coriander leaves, chopped
- 5 tablespoons walnuts, chopped
- 2 Green chills, cooped
- 1 teaspoon of Italian Mixed herbs seasoning
- Oil spray for greasing
- Salt and black pepper to taste

Directions

1. Mix all the listed ingredients into a large bowl. Make a soft dough with wet hands.

2. Shape it into nuggets and mist all the nuggets with oil spray. Add it to an air fryer basket lined with parchment paper.

3. Add the basket to the unit and close the lid. Adjust the time to 10 minutes.

4. Adjust the temperature to 400 degrees F. Flip it halfway through.

5. Once it's done, serve.

Tortillas Wraps

Prep Time: 20 Minutes

Cook Time: 20 Minutes

Yield: 3 Servings

Ingredients

- 1-1/2 cup Portobello mushrooms
- 2 sweet peppers (yellow), chopped
- 2 medium-sized onions, chopped

Ingredients for Fajita Sauce

- 4 teaspoon sweet chili sauce
- 4 teaspoon soy sauce
- 1 teaspoon smoked paprika
- 1/2 teaspoon chili powder or to taste
- 1/2 teaspoon cumin
- Salt, to taste

To serve with:

- 4 tortillas

Topping Ingredients

- Pickles, as needed
- 1 cup Guacamole
- 1 cup Salsa
- ½ cup Sour cream

Directions

1. Combine all the ingredients of fajita sauce in a bowl and set aside for further use.

2. Now chop the mushrooms, yellow peppers, and onions and add them to the sauce bowl. Place the bowl into the air fryer

3. Adjust the time to 20 minutes

4. Adjust the temperature to 400 degrees F

5. Shake the basket of the air fryer halfway through.

6. Serve over the warm tortillas, listed toppings, or any other toppings you like.

Garlic Parmesan Asparagus

Prep Time: 10 Minutes

Cook Time: 12 Minutes

Yield: 2 Servings

Ingredients

- 2 cups of asparagus
- 2 tablespoons of olive oil
- Salt and black pepper to taste
- 1/2 teaspoon garlic powder
- ½ teaspoon onion powder
- ½ cup parmesan cheese
- Oil spray for greasing

Directions

1. First, Preheat your air fryer to 400 degrees F for 2 minutes. In a large bowl, combine all the listed ingredients.

2. Toss well and transfer it to an air fryer basket lined with parchment paper. Adjust the time to 12 minutes

3. Adjust the temperature to 400 degrees F. Toss or shake the basket halfway through

4. Once done, serve with a sprinkle of grated parmesan cheese.

Sesame and Balsamic Vinegar Green Beans

Prep Time: 15 Minutes

Cook Time: 12 Minutes

Yield: 2 Servings

Ingredients

- 2 cups of green beans
- 2 tablespoons of sesame oil
- 1 teaspoon of sesame seeds
- Salt and black pepper to taste
- 1 teaspoon of balsamic vinegar
- Oil spray for greasing

Directions

1. Before starting the cooking process, preheat your air fryer to 400 degrees F for 5 minutes. Combine all the listed ingredients and toss well

2. Add it to the air fryer basket line with parchment paper. Adjust the temperature to 400 degrees F

3. Adjust the time to 12 minutes Toss the beans halfway through

4. Once done, serve and enjoy with the tossing of sesame seed on top.

Crispy Avocado Fries With Chipotle Kale Dip

Prep Time: 15 Minutes

Cook Time: 8 Minutes

Yield: 2 Servings

Ingredients

Kale Yogurt Mix Ingredients

- 2 cups kale, shredded
- 1/3 cup cilantro
- 1/3 cup plain Greek yogurt
- 2 tablespoons lemon juice
- ½ teaspoon brown sugar
- Salt and black pepper to taste
- 1 teaspoon of chipotle pepper

Other ingredients

- 2 large eggs, beaten
- 1/2 cup cornmeal
- 1/2 teaspoon garlic powder
- 2 medium avocados, peeled and sliced
- Oil spray for greasing
- ½ tablespoon of chipotle pepper

Directions

1. Before starting the cooking process, preheat your air fryer to 400 degrees F for 5 minutes.

2. Add the kale, cilantro, Greek yogurt, lemon juice, brown sugar, salt, black Pepper, and chipotle Pepper in a blender, and blend it into a paste.

3. Set it aside for further use. Whisk the egg in a small bowl.

4. Mix cornmeal, salt, garlic powder, and chipotle pepper in a large shallow bowl. Dip avocado slices in egg wash and then dredge into cornmeal mixture.

5. Layer it in oil greased air fryer basket. Add the basket to the unit.

6. Spray it with oil. Close the unit.

7. Adjust the time to 8 minutes in the air fryer Adjust the temperature to 400 degrees F. Flip the avocado slices halfway.

8. Once done, serve and enjoy with prepared kale and yogurt mix.

Spicy Herbed Zucchini Chips

Prep Time: 15 Minutes

Cook Time: 12 Minutes

Yield: 24 Servings

Ingredients

- 2 cups zucchini, sliced thinly
- 2 teaspoons of olive oil
- 2 garlic cloves, minced
- Salt and black pepper to taste
- 1/3 teaspoon oregano, dried
- 1/3 teaspoon thyme, dried
- 1 tablespoon parsley, chopped

Directions

1. Use a mandolin cutter to slice the zucchinis.
2. Before starting the cooking process, preheat your air fryer to 400 degrees F for a few minutes. Mix all the listed ingredients in a bowl and coat the squash well.
3. Transfer it to an air fryer basket lined with parchment paper. Adjust the time to 12 minutes.
4. Adjust the temperature to 400 degrees F. Flip the chips halfway through.
5. Once done, serve and enjoy.

Coated Carrots Fries

Prep Time: 15 Minutes

Cook Time: 10 Minutes

Yield: 2 Servings

Ingredients

- 1 cups of carrots, sliced thinly into sticks
- 1 cup Panko bread, crumbs
- 4 eggs
- 1/2 cup parmesan cheese
- 1 teaspoon garlic powder
- Salt and black pepper to taste

Directions

1. Before starting the cooking process, preheat your air fryer to 400 degrees F for 4 minutes. Whisk the eggs in a bowl and season it with garlic powder, salt, and black pepper.

2. Dip the carrot sticks in egg wash and dredge them into bread crumbs.

3. Add it to an air fryer basket lined with parchment paper. Adjust the time to 10 minutes

4. Adjust the temperature to 400 degrees F. Serve with a sprinkle of parmesan cheese.

Desserts

Air Fryer S'Mores Dip

Prep Time: 10 Minutes

Cook Time: 6 Minutes

Yield: 3 Servings

Ingredients

- 1 cup of chocolate chips
- 1 cup of marshmallows
- 6 Graham Crackers

Directions

1. Start by adding ½ of the chocolate chips at the bottom of a dish that can fit in the air fryer. Layer the chocolate chips with marshmallows and the remaining chocolate chips.

2. Place the dish in the air fryer.

3. Adjust the temperature to 350 degrees F. Adjust the time to 6 minutes.

4. Take the dish from the air fryer carefully and serve with graham crackers.

Air Fryer Semolina Pudding

Prep Time: 10 Minutes

Cook Time: 15-20 Minutes

Yield: 2 Servings

Ingredients

- 1 ounces semolina
- 2 cups milk
- 1 teaspoon pure vanilla extract
- 1/3 cup brown sugar, or more to taste

Directions

1. Start by mixing semolina with 1/; 2 cups of milk.

2. Once smooth, add the remaining ingredients and mix them thoroughly.

3. Once properly mixed, shift everything in a dish that fits in the air fryer and place it in the air fryer basket.

4. Adjust the temperature to 350 degrees F. Adjust the time to 15 to 20 minutes.

5. When done, take it out of the air fryer and serve either warm or cold.

Strawberry Cobbler in the Air Fryer

Prep Time: 10 Minutes

Cook Time: 15 Minutes

Yield: 2 Servings

Ingredients

- 1 box of Jiffy Golden Cake Mix
- 4 tablespoons of softened butter
- 1 can of Strawberry Pie Filling
- 1 cup strawberries, chopped

Directions

1. Before starting the cooking process, preheat your air fryer to 400 degrees F for a few minutes. Add cake mix and butter to a bowl and mix them using a fork or utensil of choice 'till a clumpy mixture is formed.

2. Add the strawberry pie filling to a 7-inch cake pan.

3. Add the clumpy cake mix over the pie filling and use a spatula to spread it over the filling evenly.

4. Shift the cake pan to the air fryer.

5. Adjust the temperature to 400 degrees F. Adjust the time to 15 minutes.

6. Wait till the top of the cake is golden brown.

7. Once brown, take it out and let it cool down for a few minutes. Top with chopped strawberries

Easy Chocolate Cake

Prep Time: 20 Minutes

Cook Time: 10 Minutes

Yield: 4 Servings

Ingredients

- 12 tablespoons of brown sugar
- 7 tablespoons of all-purpose flour
- 4 tablespoons of unsweetened cocoa powder
- 3/4 tablespoon of baking powder
- 3/4 tablespoon of baking soda
- 1/2 tablespoon of salt
- 1 large egg
- 1/2 cup of milk
- 1/4 cup of vegetable oil
- 1 tablespoon of vanilla extract
- 1/2 cup of hot water with some instant coffee powder

Directions

1. Before starting the cooking process, preheat your air fryer to 400 degrees F. Add sugar, flour, cocoa powder, baking powder, soda, and salt to a bowl.

2. In another bowl, add eggs, oil, milk, and vanilla extract and give them a mix. Mix the wet ingredients into the dry ingredients bowl, stirring slowly.

3. Then add a bit of hot water and mix a little more.

4. Shift the batter to a baking dish and place a piece of foil over it, making a few random holes. Add it to the air fryer.

5. Close the unit.

6. Adjust the temperature to 350 degrees F. Adjust the time to 10 minutes.

7. Let the cake cool for a few minutes before taking it out of the pan and serving it.

Chocolate Orange Cupcakes Recipe

Prep Time: 20 Minutes

Cook Time: 14 Minutes

Yield: 2-4 Servings

Ingredients

- 6 ounces chocolate, cut into smaller pieces
- 1 tablespoon of coconut oil
- A pinch of salt
- 1/2 cup of almond flour
- 2 tablespoons of brown sugar
- 1/4 teaspoon of orange zest
- 1 teaspoon of pure vanilla extract
- 1 organic egg

Directions

1. Adjust the temperature of the air fryer to 320 degrees F and let it preheat for a few minutes. Add coconut oil and chocolate to a bowl and melt them in the microwave.

2. Once melted, add orange zest and vanilla, and give everything a mix. Then mix almond flour, salt, whisked egg, and brown sugar in the bowl. Use silicon molds and spoon the mixture into them.

3. Arrange the molds in the air fryer basket and place a piece of foil over each mold. Adjust the temperature to 350 degrees F.

4. Adjust the time to 7 minutes.

5. After 7 minutes, take the foil off the molds and air fry it for another 7 minutes.

6. When done, take the cupcakes out and let them rest for at least 10 to 15 minutes to cool before taking them out and serving.

Air Fryer Strawberry & Cream Mug Cake

Prep Time: 25 Minutes

Cook Time: 12 Minutes

Yield: 1 -2 Servings

Ingredients

- 5 tablespoons of all-purpose flour
- 1 teaspoon of baking powder
- 4 tablespoons of milk
- 4 tablespoons of heavy cream
- 4 tablespoons of sugar
- 4 diced strawberries
- Toppings:
- Whipped cream
- Few chopped strawberries

Directions

1. Start by mixing flour, heavy cream, baking powder, milk, sugar, and diced strawberries in a bowl.

2. Coat the bottom of two ramekins with cooking spray.

3. Take the batter and fill each of the ramekins with it making sure to leave some space. Add the ramekins to the air fryer.

4. Adjust the temperature to 350 degrees. Adjust the time to 12 minutes.

5. When done, take the mug cakes out and serve with a topping of whipped cream and strawberries.

Fruit Pudding

Prep Time: 20 Minutes

Cook Time: 20-30 Minutes

Yield: 2 Servings

Ingredients

For filling

- 4 ounces of flour
- 2 ounces sugar
- 1 egg
- 2 tablespoons of milk
- 2 ounces of soft butter
- 1/2 tablespoon of baking powder

To top:

- 1 cup of fresh sliced fruit, personal choice preferred

Directions

1. Before starting the cooking process, preheat your air fryer to 400 degrees F. Mix all the filling ingredients into a bowl.

2. Keep mixing everything for at least 3 minutes so that the mixture becomes creamy and soft.

3. Shift the mixture into a baking dish, top them with fruits and toppings, and place the baking dish in the air fryer basket.

4. Adjust the temperature to 320 degrees F. Adjust the time to around 20 to 30 minutes.

5. Let the pudding cook till it is golden brown and cooked.

Lemon Biscuits

Prep Time: 22 Minutes

Cook Time: 8 Minutes

Yield: 2 Servings

Ingredients

- 1/4 cup of melted butter
- ½ cup of white sugar
- 2 cups of self-rising flour
- 2 small lemons, zest, and juice
- 2 organic eggs
- Oil spray for greasing

Directions

1. Before starting the cooking process, preheat your air fryer to 400 degrees F for a few minutes. Add all the dry ingredients to a bowl and give them a whisk.

2. In a separate bowl, mix all the wet ingredients.

3. Shift the dry ingredients into the wet ingredients and knead them till soft dough is formed. Once the dough is nice and soft, arrange it on a flat surface, and slice it into a biscuit shape. Mist the air fryer basket with oil spray, and place the biscuits onto it, keeping the space.

4. Adjust the temperature to 400 degrees F. Adjust the time to 8 minutes.

5. When done, take them out and serve.

Walnut Chocolate Cookies

Prep Time: 20 Minutes

Cook Time: 22 Minutes

Yield: 4 Servings

Ingredients

- 2 cups of all-purpose flour
- 6 tablespoons of unsweetened cocoa powder
- 2 teaspoons of baking soda
- 2/3 cup of softened butter
- 1 cup of brown sugar
- 3 eggs
- 5 tablespoons of milk
- 2 teaspoons of vanilla extract
- 8 ounces of chopped walnuts

Directions

1. Add cocoa powder, baking soda, and flour to a bowl and whisk them together. In another bowl, add eggs, sugar, and butter and mix them.

2. Then mix in vanilla and milk.

3. Once mixed, sift the dry ingredients into the wet ingredients and knead them till the dough is formed.

4. Fold some walnuts in the dough and arrange them on the baking dish. Add the dish to the air fryer basket and close the unit.

5. Adjust the temperature to 350 degrees F. Adjust the time to 16 to 22 minutes.

6. When done, take them out and serve.

Chocolate Chip Cookie

Prep Time: 20 Minutes

Cook Time: 10 Minutes

Yield: 4 Servings

Ingredients

- 2 tablespoons of softened butter
- 1 cup of brown sugar
- 2 egg yolks
- 2/3 cup of flour
- 5 tablespoons of ground white chocolate
- 2/3 teaspoon of baking soda
- 2 teaspoons of vanilla
- 3/4 cup of chocolate chips

Directions

1. Mix brown sugar and butter into a bowl and give stir until combined.
2. Once it becomes foamy, add egg yolk, flour, chocolate, baking soda, and vanilla to the bowl and mix.
3. Then mix in chocolate chips.
4. Line a parchment paper to the air fryer basket and add the batter on the parchment paper, making sure to leave at least 1-inch space at the sides.
5. Add the basket to the unit.
6. Adjust the temperature to 350 degrees F. Adjust the time to 10 minutes.
7. When done, take them out and serve.

NOTES

It's highly recommended to preheat your air fryer before starting the cooking process. Do not overcrowd the basket or rack of the air fryer.

It's not recommended to trust the time 100 percent. The way food is cut or chopped, and the portion size is the factor that affects cooking time; that's why sometimes the recommended time charts do not fit the cooking requirements.

Most food added to the air fryer must be flipped or tossed, so do not skip that step. Suitable quick read Thermometer becomes handy while preparing baked or meat items.

Conclusion

The recipes are easy to prepare and give the taste buds a roller coaster of flavors. In the end, even a beginner can fulfill their aim of creating new recipes using an air fryer. The recipes are full of nutrition and taste great. All of our recipes are loaded with nutrition and are less in fat. We highly recommend buying an air fryer for you and starting cooking today. An air fryer is one of the best alternatives to a deep fryer and even an oven. The principle of rapid air technology cooks the meal to crispy perfection. Many studies and research have shown that air fryers are the best when making a healthy alternative to deep-fried items.

As beginners, if you fear that air frying may lead to loss of texture or crispiness, then you are wrong, as this appliance is meant to make food crispy. The air fryer also has several health benefits, as you can quickly achieve weight loss goals. In addition, you can quickly lower your fat and calorie intake by cooking in the air fryer. Once you buy an air fryer for yourself, you will be amazed by it. Now, let us look at its potential benefits.

An air fryer gives you a guilt-free, healthy version of your fried foods. Here hot air circulates around the food, making it crispy, crunchy, and more nutritious. It can also be a small oven that does not heat your kitchen. The small amount of oil added during the cooking process makes the food moist and saves you from additional calorie intake. If you deep fry that same food, it will give you a day's worth of calories in one meal, which is not the case with an air fryer.

An air fryer is an efficient machine with numerous advantages. It is easy to use and operate. It does not require any complicated process for cleaning and offers easy maintenance. Your processed food tastes better if made in an air fryer, and frozen items are cooked in lesser time. Craving fried food is satisfied more healthily by cutting down the calories of fried things. Air fryers are also space-saving as they come in compact sizes and can replace your electric ovens.

Everything requires care, and so do the air fryers. Good care of your air fryer adds to its life and improves its performance. Always follow the maintenance guidelines given by the manufacturer. It is always great to have innovative, versatile, and, most important healthier ideas for cooking your everyday meals. Our cookbook has provided a great range of air-fried recipes, from breakfast to dinner, from snacks to desserts. In addition, our easy-to-follow instructions help you in preparing your required food in less time with ease. You might not have thought of making 90+ dishes in your air fryer, but we have provided numerous recipes according to need.

Our air fryer recipes will satisfy all age groups. These are not only for teenagers or youngsters who want to cut down their calories to reduce weight; or for the elderly trying to control their cholesterol. You can make your kids happy by making muffins and pizzas in the air fryer. It is the safest appliance for kids to fry their French fries and satisfy their hidden cook inside them.

Though some of the air fryers come with specified timer setups for some particular foods, still, you can adjust the time according to the recipe requirements.

To sum up, bring a healthy and happy change in your life. Add an appliance to your kitchen which is compact, time-saving, and easy to use, two in one, and best of all – a healthy alternative. Our recipes will provide you with various meals, tastes, and snacks. You will never get bored of your air fryer.

www.ingramcontent.com/pod-product-compliance
Lightning Source LLC
Chambersburg PA
CBHW050237120526
44590CB00016B/2119